The Life and Times of
QUEEN ANNE

The Life and Times of
QUEEN ANNE

Gila Curtis

Introduction by Antonia Fraser

Book Club Associates, London

*Series design by Paul Watkins
Layout by Juanita Grout*

*Printed and bound in Great Britain by
Morrison & Gibb Ltd, London & Edinburgh*

Contents

Introduction

THE LIFE OF QUEEN ANNE, last of our Stuart sovereigns, is at first sight something of a Cinderella story. After all, who would have expected in 1665, at the birth of this unimportant daughter of James, Duke of York and Anne Hyde, that she would one day come to reign over Great Britain? It seemed so remote that – as Gila Curtis writes – only a fortune-teller would have risked such a rash prediction. It was still hoped that her uncle King Charles II would have a legitimate son, and in Anne's immediate family there was already a boy and a girl older than herself to take precedence in the succession. Yet by the time Anne was thirty-seven, all these contenders to the throne had disappeared. Only her half-brother (the child of her father's second marriage) known as the Old Pretender, remained to inspire the dreams of the Jacobites. But he was a Catholic, and ever since the flight of James II in 1688, the English people had firmly rejected the direct Stuart line in favour of a Protestant monarch. On the death of Anne's brother-in-law, William of Orange in 1702, therefore, there remained only the person of this upright, conscientious, essentially English, yet shy and gout-ridden woman to represent the once powerful and fascinating House of Stuart on the throne. Now for twelve years she would preside over an age of unequalled triumphs in the sphere of war, and perhaps unequalled intrigues in the sphere of politics – the age of Queen Anne.

It is true that Anne as a character contrasted with the heroic period to which she gave her name, but for this very reason her personality has too often been overshadowed by the complicated political and social structure of the time. Anne was in many ways a tragic Cinderella, and her biography, although highly compelling in its interplay of public and private facets, certainly contained little enough of the elements of living happily ever after. Women dominate her private story, above all the famous termagant Sarah Jennings, first loved by Anne as a spirited and attractive girl, later to become the wife of her foremost soldier, John Churchill, Duke of Marlborough. This historic friendship of Mrs Morley and Mrs Freeman, as Queen and Duchess liked to sign themselves in their intimate correspondence, was itself destroyed at the hands of another woman, the subtle and outwardly submissive Abigail Masham. Yet at no point is this feminine angle irrelevant to the public politics of

Anne's reign: Whigs and Tories, and Marlborough's conduct of the war became inextricably entwined in the rival influences of Sarah and Abigail. Furthermore Anne's great personal tragedy as a woman, her inability to produce a surviving child despite seventeen pregnancies, meant that the machinations of both Whigs and Tories had to balance the possible succession of her Jacobite brother against that of the Protestant Hanoverians. Gila Curtis's achievement is to breathe proper life into her subject. By delineating warmly and at all times sympathetically Anne's emotional yet appealing nature, she enables us to get a fresh view not only of the Queen, but also of the reign itself, whose problems were so interwoven with the sovereign's own.

Antonia Fraser

Acknowledgments

Photographs and illustrations are supplied by, or reproduced by kind permission of the following. The pictures on pages 10–11, *14–15*, 16, 20, 40, 42, 68, 70, 75, 85, 91, 92, 113, 136/1, 150–1, 196–7, are reproduced by gracious permission of H.M. the Queen; on pages 26, 45, 46/1, 46/2, *48*, 118, 119, 127, *141/2*, *160/2* by gracious permission of the Duke of Marlborough. Aerofilms: 126/2; Governors of the Bank of England: 203/2; BPC: *45*, *68*, *141/2*; City Art Gallery, Bristol: *36/2*; British Museum: 18–19, 22, 31, 38–9, 54, 56–7, 60–1, 66–7, 69, 80, 86–7, 88–9, 100, 120, 124–5, *129/2*, 132/2, 135/1, 135/2, 136/2, 137, 147, 154, 162, 163, 170, 173, 178–9, 192–3, 203/1, 212; Country Life: 134, 210, 211/2; Department of the Environment (Crown Copyright): *2*, *36/1*, *141/1*; Kerry Dundas: 130–1; Fores Ltd: 150; Giraudon: 103; Ian Graham: *129/1*; Photo Hachette: 64–5; Robert Harding: *36/2*; Angelo Hornak: 213/1, 213/2; India Office Library: 186/1; Kensington Public Libraries: 77; Edward Leigh: 19; London Museum: *3*, 76–7; Longmans: *132/1*; Mansell Collection: 106; Foto Marburg: 35; Master and Fellows of Magdalene College, Cambridge: 19; National Army Museum: *110/1*, *110–111*, 122–3, 166–7; National Maritime Museum: 113–4; National Monuments Record: 126/1; National Portrait Gallery: 13, 25, 28, 43, 54–5, 73, 94, 98–9, 105, 130–1, 138/1, 138/2, 139, *144*, 156, 175, 182, 184, 189, 199, 205, 206, 207, 209, 214, 215; National Portrait Gallery of Scotland: 29, 84–5; Courtesy of the New York Historical Society: 185; Rijksmuseum, Amsterdam: 125; Royal Academy: 150–1; Royal Naval College, Greenwich: *33*; Sotheby and Co.: 151; Thomas Photos: 20, 46/1, 46/2, 118, 119, 127; Victoria and Albert Museum: 50, 51/1, 51/2, 51/3, 186/2, 187; Derrick Witty: *33*.

Picture research by Gillian Mounsey and Philippa Lewis.

DVKE AND DVTCHES OF
YORK WITH PRINCES
MAREY AND ANN

1
The
Protestant
Princess
1665-83

ANNE'S BIRTH was not a particularly noteworthy event. There were none of the celebrations – ringing of bells and burning of bonfires – which greeted royal sons. Neither Pepys nor Evelyn, the two great diarists of the age, even troubled to record it, while her father, James, Duke of York, the King's brother, in his diary made only a brief note of the exact time and date, thirty-nine minutes past eleven on the night of 6 February 1665. Charles II himself sent a characteristic letter to his pregnant sister Minette, giving her the news and wishing her more success with the sex of her own child. 'I am very glad,' he wrote, 'that your indisposition of health is turned into a great belly; I hope you will have better luck with it than the Duchess here who was brought to bed last Monday of a girl.' And he continued with his customary frankness. 'I am afraid your shape is not so advantageously made for that convenience as hers is; however a boy will recompense two grunts or more.'

The likelihood of this new-born girl ever inheriting the English throne seemed remote. Charles and his brother were still only in their thirties and both of them confidently expected to provide the nation with a family of sons. The King, in particular, had given ample proof of his fecundity, and already had seven bastards to his credit. When Anne was born he had been married to his Portuguese Queen, Catherine of Braganza, for only three years and although there were murmurings of surprise that as yet there was no sign of a royal pregnancy, few suspected that she would prove a barren wife. As for James, his wife had presented him with three children before Anne, though only two of them had survived, and there was every hope that her birth would be followed by the arrival of sons. In 1665 it would have taken a fortune-teller to predict that not only would this new niece of the King grow up to become Queen but that she would be the last of the Stuart monarchs.

Anne's parents had been married five years before, in the year of the Restoration, under a cloud of Court disapproval. They had fallen in love in France during the Stuart exile, while Cromwell's republic held sway in England, and at a time when James enjoyed a far greater popularity than he was ever to achieve in his own country. As a young man in exile he was not yet the tedious bore he became in middle age, but a good-looking Prince with impeccable manners and perfect French.

Anne's grandfather, Edward Hyde, 1st Earl of Clarendon: painted after Hanneman. For many years the chief adviser to the young Charles II, in 1667 Clarendon was dismissed from all his offices and retired abroad to write his famous *History of the Great Rebellion*.

At Versailles he was generally preferred to Charles, who was considered in comparison to be uncouth and sulky. And while his elder brother was failing to win back his throne, James had acquired a promising military reputation serving under Turenne in the French army against Spain, and had apparently succeeded in making himself 'universally beloved of the whole army by his affable behaviour'.

The object of his affections was Anne Hyde, daughter of Charles's chief minister, Edward Hyde, soon to be elevated to the earldom of Clarendon. Nevertheless, she was a commoner, and the Restoration Court was scandalised to learn that the

A birds-eye view of the palace of Hampton Court, painted during the reign of Queen Anne by Leonard Knyff. The work carried out by Wren for William and Mary on the south and east fronts and the Fountain Court can be seen in its newly-completed state. On the south side of the palace, the Privy Garden stretches to the river, while to the north lie the Melon Ground, the Wilderness and Maze, and the tiltyards which William had converted into kitchen gardens.

Miniature of Charles II, Anne's cynical but charming uncle, painted by an unknown artist during the early years of his reign.

King's brother had not only contrived to make her pregnant, but that he had secretly married her, at her father's home in the Strand, late one night before only two witnesses. Hyde himself was kept in ignorance until after the ceremony and, when he was told, his immediate reaction was that his own reputation and career would be ruined by the scandal. 'He broke out into a very immoderate passion against the wickedness of his daughter and said, with all imaginable earnestness, that as soon as he came home he would turn her out of his house as a strumpet to shift for herself and would never see her again.' In Paris the formidable Queen Mother, Henrietta Maria, was astonished that James 'should have so low thoughts as to marry such a woman' and wrote him a furious letter. As for James himself, he had completely failed to appreciate the storm that his marriage would provoke and, spurred on by an unscrupulous friend, Charles Berkeley, tried to get out of it by claiming that at least four other members of the exiled Court had enjoyed affairs with Anne in France, and that the marriage could not be valid without the King's consent. But here Charles proved himself to be more honourable than his brother, and insisted that he should acknowledge Anne as his wife and that he should ignore 'the wicked conspiracy set on foot by villains' to persuade him to desert her. James's ardour had cooled dramatically, but he finally agreed to accept his brother's advice, and within a few months Anne Hyde was accepted at Court as the new Duchess of York.

In personal terms she was more than good enough for James, who soon proved an unfaithful husband to her and turned his wandering eye on her good-looking maids-of-honour. She was more intelligent than he, and better educated than most of the ladies at Charles's pleasure-seeking Court. One of her first actions as Duchess was to patronise the Dutch artist Peter Lely and to help him to establish himself as the leading Court painter. Though not beautiful, she was held to be quite attractive until child-bearing and over-eating ruined her figure, and while she was unable to stop James's matrimonial infidelities, in other matters she was reported to lead him 'by the nose'. One of the courtiers at Whitehall summed her up neatly when he wrote, 'The Duchess has a majestic air, a pretty good shape, not much beauty and a great deal of wit.'

The male child she had been carrying at the time of her wedding lived only six months, but in 1662 a daughter, Mary, arrived, followed by a son, James, who was given the title Duke of Cambridge. By the time Anne, her third child, appeared, the growing family was comfortably installed in freshly decorated apartments in the old Tudor palace of St James's. This was an agreeable place for a London child to live, despite the fog that was constantly complained of, but Anne was not kept there for long. For the year of her birth will always be remembered as that of the Great Plague – the last visitation of that most frightening of diseases which had persistently made its appearance in England since the fourteenth century. It broke out in Drury

The garden front of
St James's Palace in the
late seventeenth century.
To the right is the
lime-avenue known as
the Mall. Engraving by
Kip and Knyff.

Lane and, during the sweltering summer, the weekly toll of
death quickly rose from hundreds into thousands. The royal
family were among those who sought refuge outside London,
and the Duke and Duchess of York accompanied the King first
to Hampton Court and then, in July, when that was felt to be
not far enough for safety, to Salisbury.

Anne escaped the Plague and the other perils of seventeenth-
century infancy, returning safely to London with her parents in
the spring of the following year, but her early childhood was to

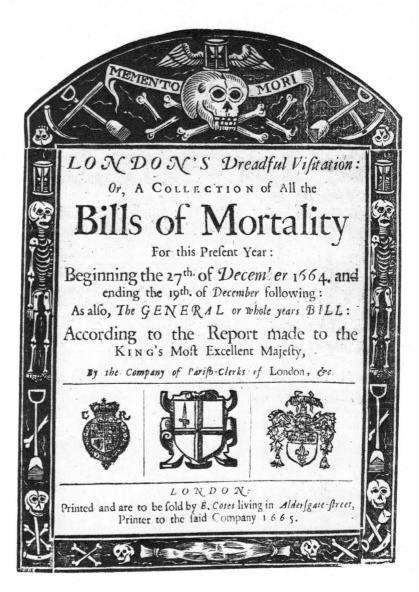

be shadowed by sickness and death among her family. In 1667 her brothers, the Duke of Cambridge and a younger boy born in 1666, both died, and another boy, born in the autumn of the same year, lived only a few hours. James's hopes of a male heir seemed destined to remain unfulfilled, for the next two children the Duchess bore him were daughters, and both of them died before they were a year old.

Anne herself was not strong. In particular she and Mary suffered from a weakness in their eyes which in Anne's case took

the form of a constant 'defluxion', or watering, and was considered sufficiently serious to send her off to consult an occulist in France when she was only four. The small child with her retinue of attendants was met at Dieppe by the coaches of her grandmother, Henrietta Maria. She spent the first few months of her visit at Henrietta Maria's palace at Colombes, until, in the summer of 1669, the widowed Queen died, and Anne was passed on to her aunt Minette, the Duchess of Orléans. It was while she was in Minette's charge that a French artist was commissioned to paint the earliest known portrait of her – a solemn heavy-faced child dressed in stiff brocade and playing with a King Charles spaniel. An audience with the French King was also thought to be appropriate for a visiting Princess, however young, and there Anne met for the only time in her life Louis XIV, whose ambitions to dominate Europe would, nearly thirty years later, be baulked by the armies of this small visitor. On this occasion Louis presented her with a pair of bracelets set with diamonds, valued at a princely ten thousand crowns.

Her stay in France was brought to an abrupt close by the sudden death of Minette, taken violently ill during the summer of 1670, almost exactly a year after Henrietta Maria's death. Her five-year-old English niece was left with no close relation at the French Court and was quickly packed off back to England to rejoin her family at St James's. In its original purpose the trip had been only a limited success for, though Anne's eyes were supposed to have improved, they continued to trouble her throughout her life and she was never able to read or write for any prolonged period without discomfort.

At almost exactly the same time that Anne was crossing the Channel back to England, Clarendon was writing a letter to her mother. In this, he demanded to know if the rumour he had heard about her was correct – that about three years earlier she had started to hold private discussions with priests of the Roman Catholic Church, and that she was now a complete convert to that faith. 'If so,' he warned her, 'you will bring irreparable dishonour on your father and your husband and ruin on your children.' But the story was true and the Duchess wrote off a spirited reply to her father, vigorously defending her decision and declaring that nothing would make her change her mind. Rumours were circulating about James's conversion

OPPOSITE Portrait of Anne at the age of four, playing with a spaniel. This painting was executed by an unknown French Court artist, while Anne was staying with her aunt, the Duchess of Orléans, to consult a French oculist.

as well, and according to his memoirs it was in 1669 that he too began 'seriously to think of salvation' and to take communion in the Church of Rome. Conversion to Rome was no small matter. Already Stuart rule had been disfigured by conflict and by open war, much of it religiously impelled. Catholicism had dangerous, irrational connotations to the broad mass of Englishmen who were never slow to recall the burning of Protestants under Bloody Mary; Guy Fawkes and his wild Catholic incendiaries; and the sinister designs of the Catholic Powers – most notably France – who, it was suspected, wished to subject all Europe to a Popish tyranny. The Duke and Duchess were, therefore, treading on dangerous ground, and in doing so set a pattern which was to shape the next reign, and, indeed, the history of the British monarchy.

But the Duchess at any rate, did not live long enough to see

Broadsheet reflecting the tremendous fears of the Roman Church and the Pope, felt in England in the 1670s.

FRom the *Romish* Whore with her Tripple Crown,   [own,
   From the Plots she hath hatch'd, and her Babes now dis-
Though they dy'd with a Lie in their mouth is well known,

these consequences, or to influence the religious upbringing of her daughters. For though she was only in her early thirties, she was already fatally ill, it is thought with cancer of the breast, and in less than a year after Anne's return from France she died. Anne was only six – probably too young to be much affected, and she said later she could not even remember what her mother looked like. But the sudden disappearance of people around her must already have become a familiar experience – first her grandmother, then her aunt, and now her mother – not to mention the fleeting lives of the little brothers and sisters in the nursery of St James's. It was a sadly appropriate beginning to a life dogged by family tragedy.

New arrangements now had to be made for the care of Mary and Anne. Charles was sufficiently realistic to accept that a Protestant education was a political necessity for his nieces, and so Lady Frances Villiers, a reliable Anglican, was selected to be their governess, and the King leased Richmond Palace to her and her husband as a suitable home. Colonel Villiers was a nephew of the first Duke of Buckingham, the ill-starred favourite of James I and Charles I, and a cousin both of the second Duke – a notorious rake at the Restoration Court – and of the King's mistress, Barbara Castlemaine. Two of his own six daughters would play an influential and not altogether happy part in the lives of the two young Stuarts now in his charge, but for the moment Richmond, with its sprawling park, fruit-filled orchard and 'handsome Bird of Turtle cage wherein Turtle Doves are kept' provided a pleasant country setting for a group of children.

Anne and Mary stayed there for most of the next three years until their father remarried, but only one small incident survives. Walking one day in the park, they started to argue whether an object in the distance was a tree or a man, Anne maintaining that it was a tree and Mary saying it was a man. When they got closer it became obvious that it was Mary who was right, but 'the Lady Anne turned away after she saw what it was, persisting still in what she had once declared, and cried, "No sister, 'tis a tree!"'

James, according to his own testimony, was an indulgent parent, and would often ride down to Richmond to spend a night or two with his daughters, arriving armed with presents.

23

But as they grew up, the religious split dividing the family was crystallising, for while the two girls were attending Anglican services under the diligent supervision of Lady Frances, it had become well known that their father was a Catholic. In 1673 Parliament passed a Test Act stipulating that anyone who refused to take the sacrament according to the rites of the Church of England should be excluded from public office, and James was obliged to resign all the official positions he held, including that of Lord High Admiral; any lingering doubts about his religious allegiance vanished.

The same year he further antagonised popular opinion, when it became known that he had selected as his second wife Mary of Modena, a Catholic Italian Princess who had only with difficulty been wooed from her desire to enter a convent. In Parliament there was an uproar, and a petition was presented to the King asking him not to allow his brother to proceed with the marriage. When this failed, a resolution was passed that the marriage should not be consummated. James's marriage seemed to threaten England with the possibility of a long line of Catholic kings, for by now there was little hope that the Queen would ever bear a child, and if James were to have a son, then this boy would take precedence over his older half-sisters. And there was no doubt that James, with his Italian wife, would make quite sure that this time any children were raised as Catholics.

But James was not to be dissuaded, and in November 1673, while effigies of the Pope were being set on fire in the London streets and rumours were circulating that she was none other than the Pope's eldest daughter, Mary of Modena arrived in England. At Whitehall at any rate she was favourably received and quickly pronounced to be both charming and beautiful. Only fifteen, she was much closer in age to her two new step-daughters than to her husband and James presented her to them as a 'new playfellow'. She was better looking than their mother had been and he was enchanted with her. She was described as 'tall and admirably shaped, her complexion was of the last degree of fairness, her hair black as jet, so were her eyebrows and her eyes, but the latter so full of light and sweetness as they did dazzle and charm too'.

It was not Mary of Modena, though, who captivated Anne at

OPPOSITE Mary of Modena, James, Duke of York's second wife, and Anne's stepmother. Portrait by Wissing, c. 1685.

24

SARAH DAUGHTER AND HEIRESS
OF RICHARD IENNINGS OF SANDRIDGE
IN THE COUNTY OF HERTFORD ESQ.
WIFE OF IOHN CHURCHILL
DUKE OF MARLBOROUGH

this time but another girl, a year younger than her new step-mother – Sarah Jennings. It is not difficult to see how a mother-less girl, overshadowed by her cleverer, more vivacious sister and by the lively Villiers daughters, would look to someone a few years older than herself on whom to fix her affections. What was to be far more unusual in Anne's case was the strength of the relationship, and the way it lasted even when she had become a middle-aged woman. Sarah was the daughter of a landed gentleman of moderate wealth and – more important – the younger sister of Frances Jennings, who had been a maid-of-honour to Anne's mother. Presumably because of her sister's position, Sarah was often at Court and she and Anne are sup-posed to have met for the first time when she was ten and Anne only five. By the time Sarah was twelve she had been given an official position among Anne's attendants and had become a firm favourite with her. Years later Sarah described the way Anne always sought her out:

> We had used to play together when she was a child and she even then expressed a particular fondness for me. This inclination in-creased with our years. I was often at Court and the Princess always distinguished me by the pleasure she took to honour me, preferably to others, with her conversation and confidence. In all her parties for amusement, I was sure by her choice to be one.

Sarah was a dazzling creature, not perhaps so classically beautiful as her elder sister, who was known as 'La Belle Jennings', but with her fair hair and blue eyes, strikingly pretty. A portrait painted by Kneller when she was in her late teens shows a confident, slightly haughty girl, with the fine straight forehead, so much admired by her husband, and well-formed features displayed to advantage by the tilt of her head. But no painter could do her justice, for it was in her sparkling vivacity and high spirits that lay the secret of Sarah's attraction. From girlhood to old age she had a radiant quality about her that was to enchant many besides Anne. In time her high spirits would turn to domineering and impatience, but she never lost the ability to charm when she wanted to, even when she was a spoilt old woman.

Her hold over Anne was a clear case of the attraction of opposites. Anne's looks were pretty enough – she had curling reddish-brown hair, pleasant if slightly plump features, and her mother's well-shaped hands of which she was always extremely proud – but she was obviously never to be a beauty. And the contrast in temperament between the two girls was even sharper. Where Sarah was always out-shining and dominating those around her, Anne was a quiet, withdrawn child, easy to overlook and painfully conscious of her own failings.

The scantiness of her education did little to help. As Sarah was later to remind her, 'Your Majesty has had the misfortune to be misinformed in general things even from twelve years old.' Women's education had returned to its customary state of neglect and Anne's schooling was very light-weight compared with the scholarly training given to Elizabeth I in the days when the New Learning of the Renaissance had earned a fashionable foothold at Court. According to Lord Peterborough, hardly one woman in a hundred could read or write, but neither he nor anyone else minded very much. Sarah herself proudly wrote, 'I am no scholar, nor a wit, I thank God!', and her secretary, Arthur Maynwaring, echoed a widespread sentiment when he declared, 'I never yet saw a lady that was the better for her education.' Anne's education was certainly no danger to anyone so minded, and centred almost exclusively on feminine accomplishments – drawing, music, French and dancing – which would enable her to play her part at Court but not to do much else.

Her religious education, though, was not neglected and her lessons on the wisdom of the Protestant faith were thorough. A devout Anglican, Edward Lake, was appointed her chaplain and tutor, and after 1675 his efforts were strengthened by the zeal of Henry Compton, a militant anti-Catholic who became 'Dean of the Chapels Royal and Preceptor to the Princesses Mary and Anne'. Constant chapel and daily prayers were routine, and by the time she had reached her early teens Anne had imbibed their teachings with a simple unquestioning faith that never left her. For the rest of her life, her belief in the superiority of the Church of England remained unshakeable.

In her other lessons she was not without talents. She had a good ear for music and was 'accounted one of the best performers on the guitar'. She also had a remarkably clear and pleasant voice, which would one day stand her in good stead when she

OPPOSITE Portrait of Anne as a young woman, just before her marriage, painted by Wissing and van der Vaart.

BELOW Henry Compton, preceptor to Princesses Mary and Anne, and later Bishop of London. It was Compton with his militant loyalty to the Church of England, not James, who was Anne's spiritual father. Portrait by Godfrey Kneller, c. 1700.

was called on to address her Parliaments. At the command of the King she was given instruction in elocution from an actress named Mrs Barry, and both she and Mary sometimes took part in the plays and masques acted at Court.

In general, though, Anne and Mary lived secluded lives apart from the dissolute atmosphere of Restoration Whitehall. They could hardly have failed to realise that both Charles and James had several illegitimate children, or that their laxity was widely emulated. But it was still assumed that royal princesses should be virtuous, and Mary and Anne passed most of their time in the company of other women or Protestant clerics. Card-playing was the only vice in which they shared, and the diversion was seized on eagerly. Anne remained an inveterate gambler all her life, but after all, what else was there to do? Sarah later recalled the boredom of those days, with the tedious talk, stuffy rooms and endless games of basset and ombre. 'At fourteen,' she declared, 'I wished myself out of Court as much as I had desired to come into it before I knew what it was.'

In 1677 the royal sisters were separated when Mary became the wife of their Dutch cousin, William of Orange, and, in floods of tears, left England for an unknown life at The Hague. But Anne was not even able to attend the wedding, for she was one of the victims of an epidemic of smallpox which had broken out in the Palace of Whitehall shortly before. For some time she was not even told that the ceremony had taken place, or that Mary had gone, in case the news made her worse. Her tutor, Lake, recorded in his diary how James 'visited her every day of her sickness and commanded that her sister's departure should be concealed from her; whereupon there was a feigned message sent each morning from the Princess to Her Highness to know how she did'. Lake himself was more concerned lest an attempt be made to undermine Anne's faith while she was ill, and he fretted over the fact that her nurse was a 'very busy zealous Catholick and would probably discompose her if she had the opportunity'. Several people died in the epidemic, including Anne's governess, Lady Frances Villiers, but Anne was more fortunate; not only did she recover, but no traces of the disease were left on her face.

But Anne's world was not to continue for long in its domestic isolation from great events. For the Court, and the country at

large, was about to be plunged into the extraordinary crisis known as the Popish Plot. There was, in fact, no plot at all; but when two inveterate liars, Titus Oates and Israel Tonge, claimed to have discovered a grand papal design to murder the King and replace him with James, the Protestant fanatics were in no mood to listen to calmer counsels. The story broke in the summer of 1678, and by the autumn had gathered its grotesque momentum. The King, ever sceptical, was powerless to stop it. Thousands of Catholics were hounded into the prisons. Several went to their death, including Edward Coleman, James's own secretary. James himself became the most unpopular man in the kingdom, and it was against his supposed influence that the Protestant mobs marched through London with their 'No Popery' banners.

There is no sign that Anne felt pity for the fate of the Plot's victims, even the members of her father's household. Rather, the horrifying tales of Catholic treason merely confirmed the lessons taught by Compton and Lake, and bore out their solemn warnings against the perils of Rome. Yet the passions of the Plot held a deep political implication, which was to transform

Edward Coleman, James, Duke of York's Catholic secretary, being dragged to his execution for his part in the Popish Plot of 1678. Woodcut from a contemporary broadsheet.

31

the character of English public life and which very nearly robbed her father of the succession. For out of the hysteria came a movement aimed at excluding the Catholic James and ensuring a Protestant monarchy. The leader of the Exclusionists, as they were known, was the intense, subtle Lord Shaftesbury, who knew well how to harness a combination of hostility to Rome, fear of French power and resentment against a lax and spendthrift Court, into an organised engine of political opposition. His followers were derisively called Whigs – the name given to Scottish outlaws – by their enemies; the Whigs in turn dubbed their opponents Tories, or Irish rebels.

But for the moment the Plot posed an immediate and painful problem : how to safeguard the legitimate succession from brother to brother. As Charles began his desperate and ultimately successful, defence of royal prerogatives, so it became clear that James's presence in England was an inflammatory luxury he could not afford. So James was ordered to leave the country, after a last hopeless attempt by the Archbishop of Canterbury to reconvert him to the Church of England. James departed with his Italian Duchess, first to Brussels and then, as High Commissioner, to Edinburgh, where he ostentatiously attended Mass and bullied the sober Scottish Presbyterians with a typical display of arrogance and insensitivity.

Altogether James was away from England for the best part of two years, and for about half that time Anne was with him, playing a rather strange role for the staunch Protestant that she was. Her six months in Brussels, then capital of the Spanish Netherlands, was to be the last time she left the British Isles. Life there passed pleasantly enough. At fifteen she was old enough to join in the social life around her and wrote home to Lady Apsley, wife of the Lord Treasurer, that she had 'gone to see a ball at the Court incognito which I liked very well. It was in very good order and some danced well enough. ... Last night again I was to see fireworks and bonfires which was to celebrate the King of Spain's wedding and they were very well worth seeing indeed.'

Anne was accompanied to Brussels by her own Protestant chaplains, and in the middle of a Catholic country she did not forget to be on her guard. To Lady Apsley's daughter, Frances, she wrote that she was never allowed to go inside a Catholic

32

church, and so could not tell her what they looked like, though she could not avoid seeing 'their images which are in every shop and corner of the street' and commented with Anglican piety, 'the more I see of those fooleries and the more I hear of that religion the more I dislike it'. Compton and Lake had done their work well.

Sarah was also in Brussels, but she did not go to Edinburgh the following year, for by then she was expecting her first baby. She had been married for over a year, though she never disclosed the precise date of her secret wedding. Her husband, John Churchill, ten years her senior, was a soldier, and their courtship had begun when he had returned to London in 1675 after fighting in the French army against the Dutch. He was completely bowled over by Sarah and the earliest letters he wrote to her show him already in love. 'My soul, I love you so truly well that I hope you will be so kind as to let me see you somewhere today since you will not be at Whitehall. I will not name any time for all hours are alike to me when you will bless me with your sight.' But Sarah was more cautious. She kept him waiting and challenged him with his affair with the King's mistress, Barbara Castlemaine. 'But on my faith,' he assured her, 'I do not only now love you, but do desire to do it as long as I live.'

It was indeed a love match and one of the most successful. When John Churchill had become Duke of Marlborough and a famous general, he was still in love with Sarah. The story was that whenever he returned from his campaigns he would 'pleasure her with his boots on'. Once when he sailed away again, he wrote to tell her how he had stood on the deck with a perspective glass in his hand 'looking upon the cliffs in the hope I might have had one sight of you.' As for her, although she gave him some trying moments, she was always totally loyal. When, after Marlborough's death, the Duke of Somerset wanted to marry her, her refusal was a proud tribute to his memory : 'If I were young and handsome as I was instead of old and faded as I am, and you could lay the empire of the world at my feet, you should never share the heart and hand that once belonged to John, Duke of Marlborough.'

Anne accepted the rival for Sarah's affections philosophically and declared that she was convinced nothing could alter their

Prince George of Hanover, Anne's cousin and her eventual successor to the English throne. His visit to the English Court in 1681 did not, however, endear him to the Princess, and, though they never met again, she retained a strong dislike of him and his family until her death.

friendship. She would content herself with 'that little corner' of Sarah's heart that still, she hoped, remained unoccupied. There was another link between her and Churchill, for John's sister, Arabella, had at one time been James's mistress, and in the strange world of divided allegiances that followed the Revolution of 1688, it would be a child of this union, Anne's half-brother and Churchill's nephew, the Duke of Berwick, who became one of England's greatest opponents on the battlefield.

Sarah, Mary, and Mary of Modena had all been married at the age of fifteen, and it was time that Anne too was found a husband. Various Protestant princes were considered by the King, but his first attempt was not a success. At Christmas 1680 Anne's cousin, Prince George of Hanover, paid a visit to the English Court, which was recovering after the traumas of the Plot. 'There was some discourse,' a contemporary recalled later, 'that he came on purpose to see the Lady Anne but that

not liking her person he left the Kingdom without making any motion to the King or the Duke of York for their consent to marry her.' The story may account for Anne's lasting dislike of George which she retained until her dying day, and which came near to jeopardising his succession to the English throne.

But whatever the reason for George's abrupt departure from Whitehall, Anne was not unattractive and she soon became the centre of a minor Court scandal by attracting the attentions of a well-known womaniser, John, Lord Mulgrave, who made what some called a 'brisk attempt' on her, though others, we are told, maintained his crime was 'only ogling'. Whatever it was, her family was alarmed. The King took practical steps to remove the danger and the unfortunate Mulgrave was deprived of all his Court offices and despatched to distant Tangiers in a leaky frigate. The gossip reached Mary in Holland and she wrote in pious distress to ask why her friend Frances Apsley had not warned her of it sooner: 'another time you will oblige me very much to let me know if there be any new ones [friendships] in hand that I may endeavour to stop it if it be not to her advantage, or at least do my best, for I think nothing more prejudicial to a young woman than ill company'.

But she did not have to worry about Anne's maidenly virtue for much longer. Early in May 1683 an audience took place at Whitehall between Charles and the Danish envoy to his Court. Shortly afterwards, Anne was informed that a marriage had been arranged between her and Prince George of Denmark, the younger brother of the Danish King, and that her future husband was expected to arrive in England for the wedding in less than three months time.

OPPOSITE ABOVE The Tower of London in about 1688: painting by Johannes Spilburg. BELOW Broad Quay, Bristol, in the early eighteenth century. Bristol, along with other West Country ports, was a thriving centre of overseas trade with America, Africa and the West Indies. Painting by an unknown English artist.

2 A House Divided

1683-88

GEORGE OF DENMARK was thirty, a big, blond man who had spent much of his adult life fighting on both sea and land against the Swedes; and whose reputation in England quickly gained a glamorous tint from the story that he had once saved the life of the Danish King, his brother, in battle. He was both good-looking and pleasant, described by one eye-witness who watched him arrive at Whitehall as 'a very comely person' with 'a few pock marks in his visage, but of very decent and graceful behaviour'. Both the King and the Duke of York were apparently satisfied with him and plans for the wedding went quickly ahead.

The marriage took place on St Anne's day – 28 July – 1683, ten days after he had landed in England. The ceremony, officiated by Anne's former preceptor Henry Compton, now Bishop of London, was held in St James's at dusk. Anne was given away by Charles, and her father, step-mother and the leading members of the Court all crowded into the small chapel to watch, while outside the palace walls the London church bells rang and the street conduits flowed with wine. The people rejoiced that George was a Protestant, even though a Lutheran and not an Anglican.

He was also dull and rather stupid. Removed from his native country – and it was taken for granted that he and Anne should live in England – and from the life of action to which he was accustomed, he never managed to carve out a proper role for himself, but remained always in the background, occupying himself by making model ships and important only because he was Anne's husband. His remarkable appetite and fondness for the bottle were the most striking things about him, and they quickly ruined his looks and sapped whatever energy he once had, turning him into a gross, rather ridiculous figure. The King's much-quoted opinion of him, 'I've tried him drunk and I've tried him sober but there's nothing in him,' was only one of a long line of Court jokes at his expense. It was Mulgrave, Anne's erstwhile admirer, who later unkindly suggested that his fits of asthma were due to the fact that he was forced to breathe hard lest he be taken for dead and removed for burial.

But in many ways George suited Anne very well, and he proved an affectionate husband to her during the twenty-five years of their marriage. She in turn became devoted to him,

The Thames at Whitehall, showing Inigo Jones's classical Banqueting Hall dominating the surrounding Tudor palace. On the left is the 'Folly' pleasure boat. Painting by an unknown artist.

loyally defending his abilities and nursing him tenderly through his many illnesses. And George's limitations had their advantages, too. He soon accepted that English politics were beyond his grasp and abandoned all attempts at influence. By the time Anne became Queen it was so completely established that his political ambitions were non-existent that his awkward constitutional position as the husband of the reigning monarch never became a controversial issue. Thus Anne was ultimately able to become the first Queen Regnant of England to combine her throne with a happy marriage.

The newly-weds set up their household at the Cockpit at Whitehall, a wedding present to Anne from the King. The building, which stood near the site of the present day Downing Street, took its name from the domed octagonal cockpit at one end, converted by Charles into a Court theatre. The apartments in the rest of the range were neither very spacious nor particularly convenient, but Anne settled down contentedly with her new husband for what was probably the happiest time of her life.

The King was now in his fifties and Restoration Whitehall well past its rakish prime, but the Court calendar was still a busy one and Anne's days sped by in a succession of balls, masques, theatres, calls and cards. Her taste for gambling could now be indulged to the full, and we hear of her playing basset with the Queen and the Duchess of York one day, and the more fashion-

able crimp in the apartments of the King's French mistress, the Duchess of Portsmouth, another. Poor George was quite bemused by the hectic pace of it all and wrote home to Denmark, 'we talk here of going to tea, of going to Winchester, and everything else except sitting still all summer which was the height of my ambition. God send me a quiet life somewhere for I shall not be long able to bear this perpetual motion.'

One friend had not been forgotten in the whirl. Marriage had done nothing to alter Anne's feelings for Sarah, and one of her first actions after her marriage was to appoint her as first Lady of her Bedchamber, which was, she wrote 'a great joy to me'. To Sarah though it was a mixed blessing. Anne was a demanding mistress, and Sarah, mother of a rapidly expanding family (within eight years she had four daughters and one dearly-

Louise de Kéroualle, Duchess of Portsmouth, who first came to England in 1670 in the train of Charles II's sister, Minette, Duchess of Orléans, but soon returned to become the King's mistress. Portrait by Mignard, 1682.

valued son, named John after his father) was inevitably absent from Court for long periods. But Anne's letters pursued her to her home near St Albans almost daily. 'I cannot do without you,' she declared, and though she wished Sarah and John 'everything your own hartes can desire', this did not mean that she thought they should remain away from London: 'you must not think that it is reasonable for you to live out of the world while I am in it'.

Ever anxious to remove any obstacle in the path of mutual affection, Anne hit upon the idea that she and Sarah should adopt the pseudonyms of 'Mrs Morley' and 'Mrs Freeman' in their letters to one another. As Sarah described later:

> For the sake of friendship (a relation which she did not disdain to have with me), she was fond even of that *equality* which she thought belonged to it. She grew uneasy to be treated by me with the form and ceremony due to her rank; nor could she bear from me the sound of words which implied in them distance and superiority. It was this turn of mind which made her one day propose to me that whenever I should happen to be absent from her, we might in all our letters write ourselves by feigned names, such as would import nothing of distinction in rank between us.

Sarah was told to choose which of the two names she preferred. 'My frank, open temper naturally led me to pitch upon Freeman and so the Princess took the other; and from this time Mrs Morley and Mrs Freeman began to converse as equals, made so by affection and friendship.'

This strange correspondence lasted for over twenty years, and in it Anne expressed, as eloquently as she could, her love for Sarah. To be without Mrs Freeman was 'a sort of Death'; Mrs Morley's 'happiness or unhappiness depends wholly on my dear Mrs Freeman'. Pseudonyms and extravagant language were the fashionable formulae of Anne's generation. In her girlish correspondence with Frances Apsley they had used the names 'Semandra' and 'Ziphares', taken from a play in which they both acted at Whitehall, and had exchanged high-flown expressions of love and devotion. But the force and sincerity of Anne's letters to Sarah break through fashionable conventions and testify to something much deeper than adolescent love. It was a relationship in which there was far more uneasy passion than in Anne's uncomplicated marriage to placid George. Her

OPPOSITE Sarah, Duchess of Marlborough, playing cards with Lady Fitzharding, formerly Barbara Villiers, and one of Anne's playmates at Richmond. Painting by Godfrey Kneller.

44

things in your letter yt I think it is better for
me not to say any things, therfore I pass them
over, & end this, wth assuring you wth ye same
sincerety I should do if I weare upon my death
bed, yt I do beleeve every thing you tell me of yt
your knowledge is true, & yt I am as tenderly
fond of you as ever, & nothing, no not your own
unkindnes, shall ever alter your poor unfortunat
faithfull Morly

Wednesday Aug ye 23

Aug ye 24, not haveing yet mett wth a safe opertunety I
think it better to send one a purpose wth this then to keep it any
longer

I must give you a thousand thanks for yt concern
you express for my safety, & sertinly if I weare
never soe weary of yt world I would take care
of my self, becaus you desire it, I do not at all
doubt of yt malice of my enemys, & shall never
be surprised to heare of plots other against my
government & my self, for it is what I expect all my
days from yt young man in France & those of his
religion, but I do promis you I will take all
reasonable care of your poor unfortunat faithfull
Morly, & more then yt life is not worth,
what you say to convince me of longpas being
falce was not at all necessary, for if you
remember when you & adored her to yt degree
yt it had almost broke my hart, I allways thought
her a Jade, as to Ld Weymouth I think I never differd

Windsor munday night Aug ye 21

I received to day when I was at dinner my dear
mrs Freemans long letter wch greives me extreamly to
find you can againe have such unkind & unjust
thoughts of me, as to beleeve me falce, & for no
reason but your telling me yt truth, oh do not
wrong me soe, I pretended I am not changed, you
have still yt same share in my hart as ever, &
I do value you more then can be exprest for telling
me your mind freely on all occasions, & when ever
you are pleased to be yt same to me as you used
to be, you will find yt same tender Morly as ever
as you did when you told me at St Jamenes you
beleeved we should never quarrel againe, do not
nurse up any hard thoughts of me becaus I
can not enter wth you into some notions as other
people can, & then I see here we shall never disagree

differd wth you, I have had a great compliment from
him, wch I take as such, & assure you I have not at
all yt better opinion of any bodys great assurances
unless I see other demonstrations of their kindnes
& what I said consercing 19 was only an answer
to what you had said of him, I hope my dear
mrs Freeman will let me have yt happynes of
seeing her before she goes to Althrop, or els
indeed it will be very cruel, & after yt Visett is
over, I beg you would com ether hither or
to yt Lody, for I can never be easy to have you
further off, & yt not long togather for upon my
word I can not live wth out you, & thus I wish you
& mr Freeman every thing your own harts can
desire, you must not think, nor no body els I am
sure can, yt it is reasonable for you to live out
of yt world, as long as I am in it. there are some

husband's devotion could always be taken for granted, but Anne was never sure of her place in Sarah's affections. It was she who, quite simply, made the running; it was Sarah who forgot to write, postponed a visit, or did not come at all. Sarah was perfectly aware of Anne's emotional dependency. Years later she wrote a description of the relationship, recording her attempts to

> ... divert and entertain and serve the Princess; and to fix that favour which now one might easily observe to be increasing towards her every day. This favour quickly became a passion; and a passion which possessed the heart of the Princess too much to be hid. They were shut up together for many hours daily. Every moment of absence she counted a sort of tedious lifeless state. To see the Duchess was a constant joy; and to part with her for never so short a time a constant uneasiness – as the Princess's own frequent expressions were. This worked even to the jealousy of a lover. She used to say she desired to possess her wholly; and could hardly bear that she should ever escape from this confinement into other company.

It is true that this was written after they had quarrelled and it is impossible to know with certainty to what extent, if at all, Anne's affection was reciprocated. At Sarah's insistence, most of her own letters to 'Mrs Morley' were burned, so that we do not even have both sides of the evidence. But it is difficult to believe that Sarah, always ambitious, ever scheming, did not make use of Anne's genuine love for her own ends, so that, in the end, we should accept that the 'affair', like the evidence, was one-sided.

If Anne had had a family of her own it might well have weakened Sarah's hold. As it was, in April 1684, her first pregnancy ended in a miscarriage and the sad story of her motherhood had begun. Eventually Anne lived through no fewer than seventeen pregnancies, leaving her with a ruined constitution and no surviving child. Even for the seventeenth century, with miscarriages a commonplace, such a record was clearly abnormal and many theories have been put forward to account for it. Some claimed that Anne had inherited syphilis from James or that it was George who was infected; others that she suffered from porphyria, a metabolic disease affecting the blood (the same malady that was later to be the cause of George III's

OPPOSITE Details from two letters written by Anne to Sarah, under the pen-name of Mrs Morley to Mrs Freeman.
Above: Anne signs herself 'your poor unfortunat faithfull Morly'.
Below: After Sarah's marriage to John Churchill, she was often absent from Court with her family. Anne's reaction was a pathetic entreaty: 'tho I wish you and Mr Freeman everything your own harts can desire, you must not think, nor nobody els I am sure can, if it is reasonable for you to live out of ye world as long as I am in it.'

47

Duke of Marlborough.

madness), and there was also talk of her having a deformed pelvis. But none of these explanations is wholly satisfactory and at this distance in time an accurate diagnosis is impossible.

Anne's maternal failure was a shattering personal tragedy. She was an affectionate, homely woman, and a young family would have happily filled the empty middle years of her life. With a family to fuss over and to plan for, Anne and George could have become a seventeenth-century Victoria and Albert, a model devoted couple presiding over a large brood. Instead only one of their children lived for more than two years; and though the young Duke of Gloucester partly filled the void, anxiety for his health always undermined the joy he brought. Yet the constant suffering, though it ruined both her health and her looks, did much to forge Anne's character; so that when she finally acceded to the throne, it was with the superior will of an invalid who has endured a full measure of suffering.

But in the first years of her marriage this strength of character was little in evidence. She remained the most ordinary of young women – as much of a nonentity as was possible for anyone in her position. On one point alone was she in any way to be identified with the great issues of State: the staunchness of her Protestantism at a moment in history when such resolution was needed. For on her twentieth birthday, 6 February 1685, her uncle Charles II died (a deathbed convert to Rome) and her father succeeded him as King. Anne was now, quite suddenly, a person of considerable consequence: second in line to the throne after her elder sister Mary, and, as a Protestant, the growing focus of those who detested the Catholicism of her father.

James II quickly showed that his religion was not to be confined to his own private life: he intended to foist it on his unwilling subjects. Any good-will generated at his accession quickly evaporated as his brief three-year reign developed like that of a man bent on political suicide. In June the Duke of Monmouth, the late King's Protestant bastard, made his ill-planned attempt to seize his uncle's throne. James's terrible revenge, characterised by Judge Jeffreys's 'Bloody Assizes' renewed all the fears of Catholic despotism and government by fire and sword. The rebellion itself was used as the excuse to create the largest standing army England had ever known, and despite the laws

OPPOSITE John Churchill, 1st Duke of Marlborough. The son of an impoverished Royalist, he had little to help him make his way in the world. But three monarchs before Anne – Charles II, James II and William – were all aware of his outstanding abilities. Portrait by Godfrey Kneller.

English Furniture in the late seventeenth century

At the beginning of the seventeenth century, craftsmen were often concerned with show when producing furniture, and even those houses which had a great amount of furniture had very few pieces which were comfortable in themselves. By 1700, this situation had completely changed: not only was there a far greater diversity in the types of furniture being made, but also greater comfort had become a major consideration in furniture design.

RIGHT English cabinet of about 1700, of walnut decorated with marquetry. By this period, cabinet-makers were using the 'carcase' of the cabinet as a base upon which to apply ornament, and thus this floral style of marquetry was enjoying international popularity. The flat platforms on the top of the cabinet were intended to hold porcelain, a fashion imported into England by Queen Mary.

ABOVE Two English armchairs of the late seventeenth century.

Left: Beechwood chair, upholstered in wool and silk embroidery. Upholstery was rarely used in England until this period.

Right: Carved walnut armchair, with caned seat and back. The carving includes the Lamb and Flaming Heart, indicating that this chair was probably used in a church.

BELOW Walnut couch or day-bed of English manufacture, c. 1680. Again this type of furniture was rarely used in England before this period.

which forbade Catholics to hold office, it was staffed increasingly by the King's co-religionists. Catholics appeared in many important positions: not only in the army and navy but in the government, while the King's Jesuit confessor, Father Petre, was ostentatiously installed in his former apartments in St James's. Parliament, naturally enough, protested; and was promptly prorogued. James was pursuing his self-appointed destiny with all the confidence of a sleep-walker.

Anne was not among those who publicly protested: it was not in her nature to do so. Her resistance was quieter, and more personal, her sights set upon peaceful co-existence. According to Sarah, she kept her Court 'as private as could be consistent with her station'. When news came of the savage punishments exacted by Judge Jeffreys, and while others were uneasily recalling the Smithfield burnings of Bloody Mary, Sarah was shocked by Anne's complete lack of sympathy for the victims – three hundred dead and strung up by the roadside as a grisly warning, and nearly a thousand more shipped off to the West Indian colonies. But it was impossible to remain completely aloof. As James surrounded himself at Whitehall with Catholics (Evelyn noted gloomily 'Romanists swarming at Court with greater confidence than ever had been seen in England since the Reformation'), so the religious aspects of daily life became a minor battlefield between him and Anne. James left religious tracts lying around her rooms and at mealtimes when he said grace, Anne made a point of talking or looking in the opposite direction. In June 1686 when she gave birth to a daughter, James promptly rushed to her bedside with a Jesuit priest.

From Holland Mary viewed the darkening situation with alarm and wrote anxiously to her younger sister. Was Anne remaining loyal to the Church in which they had both been raised? There had been reports that one of Anne's recently appointed household servants was a Catholic: was it true? It was impossible to be too careful and Anne should take care to surround herself in future only with loyal Protestants. But Mary need not have worried and the reply she received from Anne was unequivocal:

> Since you desire me to write freely on this subject, I must tell you that I abhor the principles of the Church of Rome as much as is possible for any to do, and I as much value the doctrine of the

*'I abhor
the principles of
the Church of
Rome as much as
is possible for
any to do'*

Church of England. And certainly there is the greatest reason in the world to do so, for the doctrine of the Church of Rome is wicked and dangerous, and directly contrary to the scriptures, and their ceremonies – most of them – plain downright idolatory. But God be thanked, we were not bred up in that communion, but are of a Church that is pious and sincere, and conformable in all its principles to the Scriptures. Our Church teaches no doctrine but what is just, holy and good, or what is profitable to salvation; and the Church of England is, without all doubt, the only true Church.

But Mary was not easily satisfied and demanded further re-assurances. Anne should, she insisted, report any attempt by James to convert her ; and she even went so far as to question the reliability of Sarah. Here Anne leapt promptly to the defence of her friend :

> I believe there is nobody in the world has better notions of religion than she has. It is true, she is not so strict as some are, nor does not keep such a bustle with religion ; which I think is never the worse, for one sees so many saints turn devils, but if one be a good Christian, the less show one makes it is the better in my opinion.

The correspondence was important because, for Mary at least, it went beyond the bounds of domesticity. As next in line to the throne, she and her husband provided the natural Protestant alternative, and it was in their interests to secure as many friends in high places as possible, should the day come when James be replaced by force. Not that William of Orange was anxious to invade England : he was too cautious a man to move before he was certain of success. But his whole life had been devoted to one cause, the salvation of his Protestant nation from the armies of Louis XIV, and it was not to be imagined that he would sit idly by while England ranged herself alongside the Catholic powers. And so he kept in touch, his agents busily testing the strength of Protestant feeling in England and passing back the information to their master.

It is impossible to say when Anne became aware of the likelihood of William's invasion. There is no doubt, however, that when it happened she was fully prepared. William's agents certainly made contact with her, and it is safe to assume that far more passed between them than she dared commit to writing. Even so, by 1687, her letters to The Hague were taking on an increasingly conspiratorial tone. The sisters used code-names

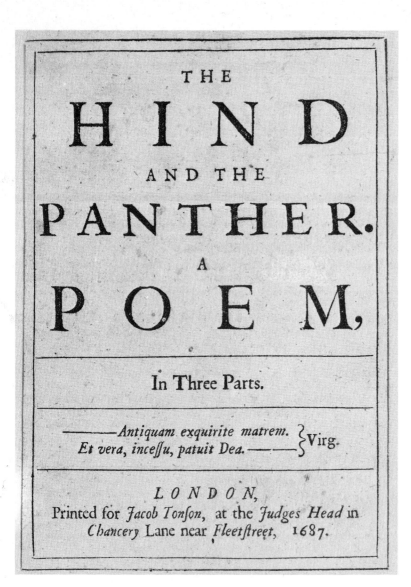

THE

HIND

AND THE

PANTHER.

A

POEM,

In Three Parts.

———— *Antiquam exquirite matrem.*
Et vera, inceſſu, patuit Dea. ————} Virg.

LONDON,
Printed for *Jacob Tonſon,* at the *Judges Head* in
Chancery Lane near *Fleetſtreet,* 1687.

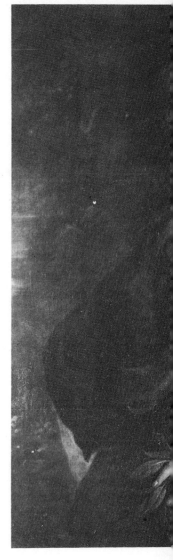

and Anne was at pains to make sure that only the most trust-worthy messengers were employed.

In her dilemma it was naturally enough to the Churchills that Anne looked for guidance. Though she had no qualms about the direction she should take, the intricacies of conspiracy needed a more sophisticated touch than she felt capable of. Churchill's own position was not unlike Anne's, for he owed much to James but, like her, was deeply distressed by James's course of action. In many ways, though his position was com-

John Dryden was Poet Laureate to both Charles II and James II. He had been outspoken in his attacks against Shaftesbury and the Whigs during the period of the Popish Plots, and in 1687 wrote a poem for Roman Catholicism, entitled *The Hind and the Panther.*

54

plicated by personal ties, he represented the moderate men to whom James, had he been concerned to keep his throne, should have looked for his advisers. Churchill was clearly able, a man of common sense with growing wealth to make him cautious, certainly not one lightly to commit himself to the uncertain course of overthrowing his King. In religion he was far less zealous than Anne, though more devout than Sarah. Yet it was precisely this group of moderate influential opinion that James was alienating. When William's agent, Dykevelt, came over to England, Churchill quickly took the opportunity to write a letter to William 'to give you assurances under my own hand that my places and the King's favour I set at nought in comparison of being true to my religion'.

For Anne, 1687 was a year of personal as well as political stress. In January she again miscarried due, she believed, to dancing the rigadoon, a new French dance which required a good deal of jumping. Then in February, within a week of each other, she lost her two infant daughters, Mary born in 1685 and Anne Sophia born in 1686. George, too, was sick and Anne mourned by his bedside. 'I never heard any relation more touching than seeing them together,' wrote one of the ladies at Court, 'sometimes they wept, sometimes they mourned in words, but hand-in-hand, he sick in his bed, she the carefullest nurse to him that can be imagined.' It was beginning to seem as if the Stuarts were fated in their inability to produce heirs. In Holland, after several miscarriages, Mary still had no children, and in England James's Queen had not had a pregnancy for three years. After all the alarms at the time of James's marriage, it now looked as if his policies would die with him. Then, at the end of the year, came the announcement from the Palace that the Queen was with child and that it was expected the next summer. At once there was consternation throughout the country, as the implications of an unending Catholic dynasty were grasped.

Anne shared fully in the dismay. The Tuscan envoy in London wrote home that he was quite unable to find the words to express 'the fury of the Princess of Denmark at the Queen's condition'. Anne's friendship with her step-mother had long since vanished. She had already acquired the impression that it was the Queen who 'pressed the King to be more violent than he would be of himself; ... for she is a very great bigot in her

LEFT The title-page to the poem. The Hind, immortal and unchanging, represents the Roman Church, and the Panther the Protestant Church. ABOVE Kneller's portrait of Dryden, painted in 1693.

The King's and Queen's
baths at Bath in 1675.
Anne and George
frequently visited Bath to
take the waters.

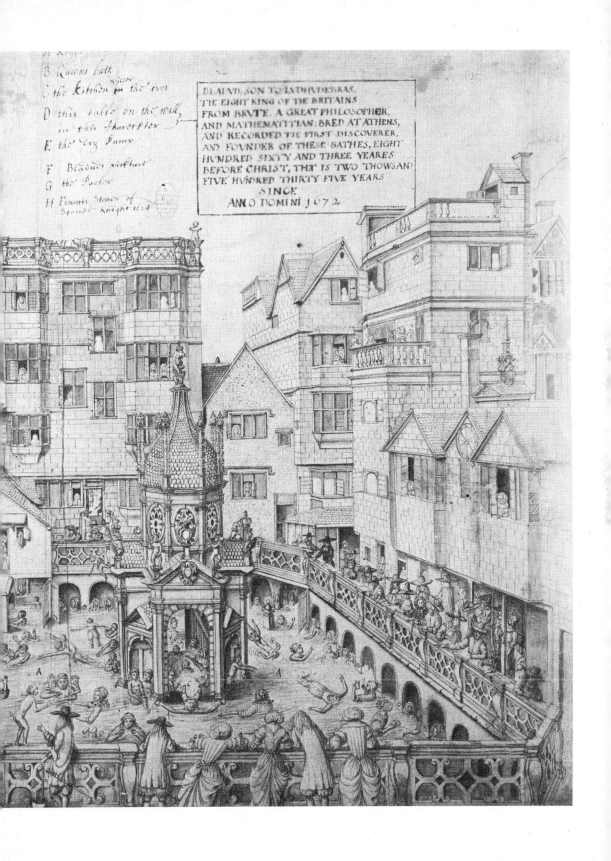

B Queens bath
C the Kitchin vnder the ius
D this table on the wall, in this Shorofter
E the Dry Pumx
F Bladuds wichout
G the Paulor
H Francis Stoner of Stoner Knight 1624

BLADUD, SON TO LVDHVDEBRAS,
THE EIGHT KING OF THE BRITAINS
FROM BRVTE, A GREAT PHILOSOPHER,
AND MATHEMATITIAN: BRED AT ATHENS,
AND RECORDED THE FIRST DISCOVERER,
AND FOVNDER OF THESE BATHES, EIGHT
HVNDRED SIXTY AND THREE YEARES
BEFORE CHRIST, THAT IS TWO THOWSAND
FIVE HVNDRED THIRTY FIVE YEARS
SINCE
ANNO DOMINI 1672

way, and one may see by her that she hates all Protestants'. Now criticism turned to open vindictiveness. It was rumoured that the Queen's pregnancy was a false one, nothing but a sinister plot to foist a Catholic heir on the nation, and Anne eagerly took up the idea. In March 1688 she wrote to Mary in Holland:

> I can't help thinking [the Queen's] great belly is a little suspicious. It is true indeed she is very big, but she looks better than ever she did, which is not usual: for people when they are so far gone, for the most part look very ill. Besides it is very odd that the Bath, that all the best doctors thought would do her a great deal of harm, should have had so very good effect so soon, as that she should prove with child from the first minute she and Mansell [James] met, after her coming from thence. Her being so positive it will be a son, and the principles of that religion being such that they will stick at nothing, be it never so wicked, if it will promote their interest, give some cause to fear there may be foul play intended. I will do all I can to find it out if it be so: and if I should make any discovery, you shall be sure to have an account of it.

Anne was evidently as good as her word, and did her best to catch the Queen in a state of undress. But, not unnaturally, Mary of Modena recoiled sharply from her prying, and even, on one occasion, was driven to throwing her glove at Anne when her curiosity became too tiresome. A week later Anne took up her pen to report again to Mary:

> Whenever one talks of her being with child she looks as if she were afraid one should touch her. And whenever I happen to be in the room as she has been undressing, she has always gone into the next room to put on her smock. These things give me so much just cause for suspicion that I believe when she is brought to bed nobody will be convinced it is her child, except it prove a daughter. For my part, I declare I shall not, except I see the child and she parted.

But Anne was not to be a witness to the birth. As the Queen's pregnancy entered its last phase, Anne was to be found, surprisingly, not at her side, but taking the waters at Bath. Certainly her absence was considered odd at the time. 'I much wonder,' wrote Lady Bridget Noel, one of the ladies at Court, 'the Princess of Denmark would not compliment the Queen and see her safely delivered before she went to Bath.' Possibly domestic cares pushed out political ones. George's asthma was always helped by a visit to Bath, and Anne herself may have wanted a change of scene after yet another miscarriage – her fourth – in April. One can only conjecture as to the reasons but, whatever they were, her absence in Bath meant that when Mary of Modena went into labour at eight o'clock in the morning of 10 June, Anne was not present among the great numbers summoned to the lying in at St James's. Afterwards she maintained that the baby had originally been expected a month later, and that it was precisely because she was away from London that the date had suddenly been brought forward.

It seems incredible that a birth which took place while the Lord Chancellor, the Queen Dowager, most of the Privy Councillors, and at least twenty women were all in the room, should have continued to be the subject of wild rumours. Yet such was the atmosphere of suspicion against James that Anne was probably right when she said that only the birth of a daughter would quash the idea that the baby was not the Queen's. And the baby was not a daughter. Instead the Queen was delivered of a fine healthy boy, and all the Protestant fears seemed confirmed. It was, simply, too bad to believe, and so they did not believe it, preferring the story that the baby had been smuggled into the childbed inside a warming-pan an hour or so before the 'birth'. It was a fantastic idea which nobody now accepts; but Anne, along with many thousands of her fellow-countrymen, eagerly subscribed to it. 'My dear sister,' she wrote to Mary, 'can't imagine the concern and vexation I have been in that I should be so unfortunate to be out of town when the Queen was brought to bed, for I shall never now be satisfied whether the child be true or false. It may be it is our brother but God only knows. . . .'

> '*It may be that it is our brother but God only knows*'

James, of course, was delighted at long last to have a son. He knighted the doctor, gave the midwife a purse of five hundred guineas 'for your breakfast' and that evening wrote a fulsome entry in his diary – very different from his terse record of Anne's own birth twenty-three years before. But in fact the birth was one of the last steps towards his ruin. William of Orange shortly received two letters from England, one from James, cheerfully reporting the arrival of 'a very strong boy', and another giving him the signal he had been waiting for. Seven of the leading men in England, including Compton, formally invited him to lead a rising against James.

Engelants schouwtoneel, verbeeldende het vlugte van Iacobus II.
Koning van Groot-Britanyen etc. met deffelfs aankomst in
Yrlant en verdere voorvallen.

tot Amsterdam by Adr: Schoenebeek in de kalverstraat

Le Theatre d'An
Roy de la grana
autres avantures

Engraving glorifying the arrival
of William and Mary in
England in 1688, and
James II's subsequent flight.

60

After this signal William needed only a few more months to complete his plans, and early in November he landed with a small force at Torbay. James, at this critical moment, was indecisive. A quick stroke might have succeeded, but the King dithered in London while William gathered support. Finally he left his capital to assemble his troops at Salisbury, leaving with the Bishop of Ely the ironic message that if anything should happen to him, care should be taken to break the news to Anne, who was again pregnant, very gently. The following day, 18 November, Anne wrote to William:

> I shall not trouble you with many compliments, only in short assure you that you have my wishes for your good success in this so just an undertaking, and I hope the Prince [George] will soon be with you to let you see his readiness to join with you. ... I am not yet certain I shall continue here or remove into the City; that shall depend on the advice my friends will give me, but wherever I am I shall be ready to show you how much I am your humble servant.

Anne's and George's desertion was, of course, to be co-ordinated with the Churchills', and it was John Churchill who was the first of the four to come into the open against James. On the night of 23 November, he stole away from the camp at Salisbury, taking some four hundred troops with him and rode off to join William. A few days later George followed, a defection not much lamented by James, whose only sour comment was supposed to have been that the loss of a single trooper would have been of more consequence. But by that time James's situation was desperate. In the north, in Yorkshire, Cheshire and Derby, Danby, Charles II's former minister, the Earl of Devonshire, William Cavendish, and Lord Delamere were raising other armies against him, and news was coming in that the fleet under Lord Dartmouth was also moving over to William. A fight seemed hopeless, negotiation was not seriously considered and, not knowing what else to do, James turned back towards London.

This was the last thing Anne had expected or wanted. According to Sarah, news of her father's return put Anne into a 'great fright', and she told her that rather than see him she would 'jump out of the window'. Indeed, she lost no time in making her escape. That same night, after midnight, with Sarah and one of her other ladies, Anne crept down the backstairs from her closet to a pre-arranged meeting place with Henry Compton and his nephew, the Earl of Dorset. No one saw them go, and the only casualty was one slipper, which fell off in the mud. The rest of the night was spent at Compton's palace in the City and from there early next day, still undetected, they set out northwards to join the forces rising for William under Cavendish. As they moved away from London their flight turned into a triumphal progress. In the villages and towns along their route Anne was hailed as the Protestant Princess and greeted by demonstrations of loyalty. By the time they reached Market Harborough, she was surrounded by a growing band of volunteers with Compton, who in his youth had been a cornet of dragoons, riding at their head, a drawn sword in one hand and pistols on his saddle, probably having the time of his life.

Meanwhile, at Whitehall, the discovery of her flight had caused 'a universal outcry among the ladies that some or other had carried away the Princess'. Anne's old nurse, Mrs Danvers, had gone in to her room to call her and, receiving no answer, 'she opened the bed and found the Princess gone and her bed cold, with all her yesterday's clothes even to her stockings and shoes left behind . . .'. James reached London that evening and the news cut him to the heart. 'God help me!' he cried, with tears running down his cheeks, 'Even my children have forsaken me!' There was little consolation for him in the stilted letter of explanation which Anne had left behind addressed to the Queen:

> Never was anyone in such an unhappy condition, so divided between duty and affection to a father and a husband; and therefore I know not what I must do, but to follow one to preserve the other. I see the general feeling of the nobility and gentry who vow to have no other end than to prevail with the King to secure their religion, which they saw in danger by the violent counsels of the priests; who to promote their own religion, did not care to what dangers they expose the King. I am fully persuaded that the Prince of Orange designs the King's safety and preservation, and hope all things may be composed without more bloodshed, by the calling a Parliament. God grant a happy end to these troubles, that the King's reign may be prosperous, and that I may shortly meet you in perfect peace and safety; till when, let me beg of you, continue the same favourable opinion that you have hitherto had of your most obedient daughter and servant.

Anne never saw her father again. While she waited, first in Nottingham and then in Oxford, William marched steadily towards London and James's thoughts turned to flight. He sent his wife and baby son to France in the second week of December and then, with his illegitimate son Berwick, and three other companions, on 23 December, he too left England in a fishing-smack for the second long exile of his life. This time it was to be permanent.

Anne voiced no regrets when she heard the news. Whatever their faults, her hostility to James and her step-mother was un-attractive. But the prejudices which sustained her feelings were shared by many other English men and women and it was these which ultimately drove James from his throne. Like so many others, Anne saw the issue in crude religious terms and her acceptance – part opportune, part sincere – of the more un-likely tales that helped to rob James of his reputation, only reflected the gossip in the streets outside. As so often in the future, it was Anne's very limitations, her lack of imagination, that enabled her to echo the national mood far more closely than most of her Stuart predecessors. Yet, during the long years of middle age to come, she would have plenty of time to reflect on her betrayal of the man who was not just a Catholic, but her King and her father, and on her behaviour towards the spirited Italian woman whom she had so eagerly cast in the role of un-scrupulous plotter. Anne kept her feelings towards James and his son to herself, remaining stolidly opposed to the idea of another Catholic King of England. And yet, 'maybe tis our brother'. She would never openly admit it, but the doubt was there, perhaps to trouble her for the rest of her life.

3 Waiting in the Wings 1688-1702

As JAMES'S ROYAL BARGE slipped away down the Thames in a rainstorm, William of Orange made his entrance into London from the West, avoiding the expected route and the damp crowds lining the streets with orange ribbons fluttering from their hats. But inside St James's Palace, throughout the night and all the following day, he listened to the congratulations and acknowledged the gratitude of the Protestant clergy, and civic dignitaries who welcomed him as their nation's saviour.

Yet William was ill-suited to the role of England's hero. The solitary, burning ambition of his life remained the destruction of French power and the removal of the threat hanging over his beloved Netherlands. For England herself he felt no great love or sympathy ; and for their part the English came to regard him as an ungracious figure. John Evelyn's first impression of him was 'very stately, serious and reserved' ; and a month later he was complaining of the 'morose temper of the Prince of Orange who showed little countenance to the noblemen and others, who expected a more gracious and cheerful reception when they made their court'. Compared with Charles and James, he was indeed unimpressive, with his puny, almost deformed body and his thin white face pitted from smallpox. He worked hard though, with the result that he was constantly in a state of exhaustion. His Scottish chaplain, Bishop Burnet, wrote of him : 'He was always asthmatical, and suffered from a constant deep cough. His behaviour was solemn and serious, he spoke little and most commonly with a disgusting dryness.'

In the months following James's flight the situation in England remained confused. William had invaded not as a rival claimant to the throne but to protect 'the Protestant religion and the liberties of the subject' – as the motto embroidered on his standard proclaimed – and few people expected him to become King. If James had remained in England and had agreed to a programme of concessions he could well have kept his Crown, but his sudden and unexpected flight to France brought the country to the verge of chaos, as soldiers from his disbanded army roamed and plundered the countryside. It was apparent that the vacuum at the centre had to be filled, and in January 1689 a Convention Parliament addressed itself to the question of William's position in the country.

The problem was a difficult one, for James's hereditary right

66

PREVIOUS PAGES
William and Mary as the champions of freedom.

Receptie van S.K.H. den H.Prince van Orange op zyn intrede tot Londen

The Reception of His Royal Highness the Prince of Orange at his entring London

R. de Hooge fecit.

ABOVE At Christmas 1688, William of Orange entered London. This engraving by de Hooghe shows William, with his army at his back, being welcomed by the chief citizens of London. Behind is the city of Westminster and the palace of Whitehall.

67

to the throne was unquestionable, and even if his flight was interpreted as abdication then, according to the normal laws of succession, the throne should pass to Mary and not to William. Should William be made the Queen's Consort, Regent, King by himself, or joint monarch? The High Tories favoured the idea of a Regency with James still retaining the formal title of King, but with William acting for him, which was a solution that was less of an affront to the sanctity of kingship and to their own consciences. A small group led by Danby thought Mary alone should become Queen, while the old Exclusionist Whigs backed William and applauded the prospect of a King who so clearly owed his title to Parliament rather than God. But it was William's own refusal to become his 'wife's gentleman usher' that finally produced the famous compromise by which, on 13 February in the Banqueting Hall at Whitehall, the Crown was offered jointly to William and Mary.

It was a compromise devised to meet the needs of the moment, but it was one which transformed the character of the British monarchy. No future sovereign was ever able to claim,

OPPOSITE William Wissing's portrait of William of Orange, painted in 1685 for his father-in-law, James II.

BELOW Political satire of 1690. The Protestant Grindstone: William Sancroft, the Archbishop of Canterbury, and Henry Compton, the Bishop of London, turn the stone, grinding the Pope's nose, while William and Mary look on. To the left stand Jesuit priests, and to the right William's Dutch followers, led by the Count Schomberg.

as the earlier Stuarts had done, that they ruled by Divine Right and were responsible for their actions only to God. The fact that the legitimate succession had been broken was, by itself, a blow to the sanctity of kingship second only to the execution of Charles I, but in the early years of William and Mary's reign Parliament drove home its advantage by passing a series of laws defining and limiting the powers of the Crown and plainly subjecting it to the supremacy of both Statute and Common Law. The prerogatives and influence of the monarchy were still considerable, but never again would a British sovereign try to suspend, as James had done, the operation of a law, or dispense with the statutory penalties of an Act of Parliament.

In these negotiations Anne played no part; but in the plans for the succession her consent was essential. After Mary she was next in line, and had a far stronger claim than William himself; but in the event of Mary dying before William, she was now asked to waive her rights in William's favour until his own death. This could well have meant that she would never become Queen, and at first Anne – always sensitive on matters touching her hereditary rights – had doubts. She informed her uncle Clarendon that she could never consent to anything that was to the prejudice of herself and her children, and Sarah, ever at her elbow, was urging her to be firm. Sarah had a low opinion of William and had been taken by surprise at the idea he should become King; and as for the notion that Anne should not succeed Mary directly, 'at first I did not see any necessity for such a measure; and I thought it so unreasonable that I took a great deal of pains (which I believe the King and Queen never forgot) to promote my Mistress's pretentions'. For once, however, Sarah did not get her way; Anne's consent, after a little persuasion, was given, and by March she wished it to be known that she was extremely pleased by the new arrangements.

In February, when Mary arrived from Holland, there had been a joyful reunion between the two sisters. Anne and George went down to Greenwich to meet her, and the three of them travelled back by river to Whitehall where William was waiting. Mary, now twenty-nine, was tall and good-looking. Her natural vivacity had, it is true, been somewhat curbed by her harsh treatment from William, who paid her little attention and who even went so far as to instruct her to bring over his

OPPOSITE Mary II, when Princess of Orange, painted by William Wissing as a companion portrait to William, reproduced on page 68. Wissing was sent to Holland in 1685 at the command of James II to execute these portraits.

mistress, Elizabeth Villiers – her old playmate from Richmond – with her when she came to England. But to several onlookers, Mary's unrestrained behaviour on arrival at Whitehall showed a disconcerting lack of respect for her father, whose palace this had been such a short while before. Evelyn described her as coming 'laughing and jolly as to a wedding', while Sarah maintained succinctly that 'she wanted bowels', by which she meant sensitivity.

Anne spent the first summer of the new reign with William and Mary at Hampton Court, which William found far better for his asthma than St James's or Whitehall; and which, besides, reminded him of his Dutch palaces for which he felt homesick. Anne's pregnancy was by now well advanced, but as the months passed and the baby did not appear her doctors began to wonder if she was not simply ill with dropsy. It was her seventh pregnancy and so far only her two daughters had been born alive, all the others ending in stillbirths or miscarriages; and after all the strains of the previous winter it is amazing that this one did not go the same way. But when, on 24 July, Anne was safely delivered of a son, her joy is easy to imagine. And politically, too, it was an important event. For it meant that there was now a prince to ensure the Protestant succession and to offset the threat posed by James's year-old son. William and Mary by now had little hope of children of their own and Anne's boy was quickly acknowledged as the heir of the next generation. He was tactfully christened William after the new King, who stood sponsor to him at the font, and shortly afterwards gave him the title of Duke of Gloucester.

But to everyone's distress it soon became apparent that Gloucester was a delicate baby and there were many predictions that he would quickly follow Anne's other children to the grave. He refused to take his milk and had terrible fits of convulsions which no one could stop. As he steadily lost weight an anguished search was made for a wet nurse who could get him to suck. The wife of one of Prince George's footmen was briefly installed, but dismissed when it was discovered that she had lied about 'the freshness of her milk'. New applicants were sent for, each reject receiving a fee of five guineas to encourage other candidates; and it was George who picked Mrs Pack, a woman from Kingston who, though horribly dirty and

OPPOSITE Anne with her son, William, Duke of Gloucester: portrait by Godfrey Kneller, c. 1694 when Gloucester was about five years old.

72

described by one of the doctors as more fit for a pigsty than a prince's bed, proved miraculously successful. The Prince's fits ceased within a matter of hours, and he was soon putting on weight satisfactorily.

Even so, his parents continued to worry about him. He was clearly not strong and, as he grew, a curious swelling developed on his head. No one knew what it was, though the doctor's solution of piercing it at intervals to draw off the fluid inside seemed to work. Today it is thought that Gloucester had hydrocephalus, or water on the brain, a disease which, untreated, usually kills children within four or five years. It is, therefore, surprising that he survived until the age of eleven, and, while he lived, Anne's constant anxious references to her 'poor boy', her concern that he should have the best possible attention, and her touching pride as he grew from a baby into an intelligent, high-spirited boy, make pathetic reading.

To add to Anne's woes came a rapid deterioration in her relations with William and Mary. The joyful reunion between the two sisters was followed by a realisation that after ten years apart they were, in fact, strangers. The mutual affection expressed so often in their letters and heightened by the thrill of conspiracy did not prove able to stand up to prolonged contact. Sarah believed that the trouble was partly due to their difference in temperament and that 'Queen Mary grew weary of anybody who could not talk a great deal and the Princess was so silent that she rarely spoke more than was necessary to answer a question.' William's opinion of Anne fanned his wife's irritation with her. He remarked to one of his friends that if he had had to marry her instead of Mary, he would have been the most miserable creature on earth, and he made no attempt to please her, often indeed ignoring her completely. Anne confided to Sarah how once, when she was dining with him and Mary, William ate a dish of spring peas without offering any to her. Anne confessed that 'she had so much mind to the peas that she was afraid to look at them and yet could hardly keep her eyes off them.'

A serious quarrel broke out with William over Anne's allowance. She wanted an official State grant, formally voted by Parliament, rather than a gift made from William's own income at his pleasure. Again it was Sarah who set herself to promote Anne's interests, exerting her influence in Parliament to get the grant supported. Pressure was brought to bear by William, who threatened that Sarah's intervention would jeopardise her husband's career. When this tactic failed, Anne herself was approached via the Earl of Shrewsbury, promising that William would grant her £50,000 a year if she would drop the idea of a Parliamentary allowance. But Anne was showing that once she had set her mind on something she was not easily shaken, and in the upshot it was William who, to his considerable annoyance, met defeat, the episode ending with Parliament voting Anne an annual income of £50,000, Sarah's efforts were duly rewarded by her grateful mistress who offered her £1,000 a year. Anne, for all her faults, was never mean with money, and to Sarah and John her generosity was bottomless.

Not surprisingly, Anne's relations with William and Mary grew worse in the aftermath of the affair and here William's treatment of Prince George did not help. In the spring of 1690 William departed for Ireland, where James had landed with a French army, and George, seeing the chance of active service

Prince George of Denmark, riding on horseback along the shore. He wears military dress with the Garter ribbon over his breastplate, while in the background lie the ships of the fleet. This portrait was painted by Michael Dahl in 1704, presumably in connection with the Prince's ambitions to become 'Generalissimo'.

again, went along with him. For William the expedition was a
complete success and in August he roundly defeated James at
the Battle of the Boyne, forcing him once more to flee to France.
But for George, the campaign was a total flop. He had equipped
himself at considerable expense and, as William's brother-in-
law, naturally expected to be given a key post in the army. But
William took no more notice of him than if he had been 'a page
of the back stair', refusing even to allow him to travel in the
same coach, and at the end of the summer George returned to
England angry and hurt.

While their husbands were away confronting the enemy and
each other, the friendship between the two sisters had been
outwardly patched up. In April Anne visited Mary to apologise
for the trouble over the allowance; at which Mary claimed to be
delighted and assured Anne that, as far as she was concerned,
nothing would ever impair their relationship again. That
summer Anne accompanied her sister when she reviewed the
troops at Blackheath, and later they together inspected Campden House which Anne was considering for Gloucester, who
seemed to benefit from the Kensington air.

But much damage was done to her relations with the King
and Queen by her friendship with the Churchills. When she had
been in Holland, Mary had professed herself to be very fond of
Sarah and had often written to her or sent her affectionate

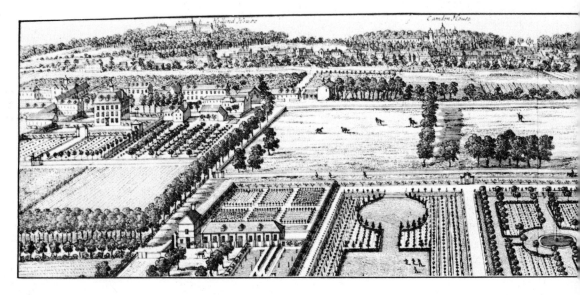

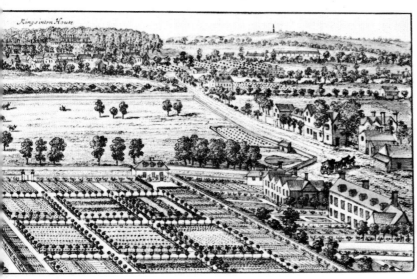

In 1690 Anne decided to purchase Campden House in Kensington for her delicate son, Gloucester. ABOVE Campden House, as it appeared in 1647: engraving by Wenceslaus Hollar. LEFT The village of Kensington, showing, left to right, Holland House, where William and Mary lived while Kensington House was being built, Campden House, the home of Princess Anne, and Kensington House.

messages through Anne. But once she had arrived in England her cordiality quickly disappeared and, particularly since Sarah's intervention over Anne's allowance, Mary became convinced that she was exerting an evil influence. The issue extended beyond personal dislike, for Anne's association with the Churchills carried with it potential danger to the Crown. By herself Anne was almost powerless; but with the Churchills to back her there was a distinct possibility that she might become a focus of opposition.

Exactly what the threat amounted to is, and will remain, unknown. William had his suspicions, but then he was a suspicious man. It was almost inconceivable that the Churchills could, with Anne, have contemplated open opposition and support for James's restoration. Yet Churchill, though William had created him Earl of Marlborough for his support in 1688, was certainly among those eminent Englishmen who maintained their contacts with James, and he was able to use his nephew Berwick as one channel of communication, and Sarah's sister, a fervent Jacobite, as another. He also saw some of the Jacobite agents who busied themselves in England trying to build up support for James. But his real intentions are obscured by his own elusive personality and also by the nature of the evidence. For the Jacobites constantly exaggerated the extent of their support in England both to bolster up their own hopes and to convince Louis XIV that their cause was worth supporting. Probably Marlborough was doing no more than many others – just trying to obtain a pardon from James and insuring his position against any future restoration. But he had grown increasingly dissatisfied with his treatment under William. He had expected some recognition for his support and like George – only with rather more merit to justify his case – hoped for some important military command. But, though he served under William in Ireland and in Flanders, the expected advancement was not forthcoming, and instead he found himself pushed aside for William's Dutch followers. One contemporary described how he never saw Englishmen dining with the Prince of Orange, but only Dutchmen. Clarendon and Marlborough were often in attendance but were dismissed when dinner was only half over. It was hardly a tactful way to behave towards someone so influential and ambitious and, as English dissatisfaction with William grew, Marlborough became one of his most outspoken critics, opposing his conduct of the war against France and his grants of Crown property to Dutchmen, and organising formal addresses in Parliament against the employment of foreigners. His behaviour so goaded William that he said openly at Court that if he were not a King, 'he would have felt it necessary to demand personal satisfaction'.

And what of Anne? Among her correspondence is a letter dated 1 December 1691, to her father:

> I have been very desirous of some safe opportunity to make you a sincere and humble offer of my duty and submission to you, and to beg that you will be assured that I am both truly concerned for the misfortune of your condition and sensible, as I ought to be of my own unhappiness. As to what you may think I have contributed to it, if wishes could recall what is past, I had long since redeemed my fault. I am sensible it would have been a great relief to me if I could have found means to acquaint you earlier with my repentant thoughts, but I hope they may find the advantage of coming late, of being less suspected of insincerity than perhaps they would have been at any time before.

This is scarcely the stuff of treason: yet it is a dramatic change of attitude from the days of her defection. The threat she posed to William and the extent of her collusion with the Churchills are clouded with uncertainty. But William would have recognised the possibilities summarised by Winston Churchill, Marlborough's great biographer and descendant, in a purple phrase: 'In Parliament, the Army and the Princess Anne a fatal trident – in the hands of Marlborough, pointed at his heart.'

It is this trident which helps to explain the bitter quarrel that was about to break out between William and Mary on one hand and Anne and the Churchills on the other. Anne's personal relationship with her sister and brother-in-law had never properly recovered from the fight over her allowance. Mary, preoccupied and miserable with life in general, found her unbearably irritating while, for her part, Anne was running an ill-natured vendetta against William, who was well aware that at the Cockpit he was known by a variety of unflattering nicknames, such as 'Caliban', 'The Dutch Abortive' and 'The Monster'. Early in 1692 the feud erupted into the open when Mary sent for Anne. News had reached her of Anne's £1,000 a

'In Parliament, the Army and the Princess Anne a fatal trident'

79

V Aliant Protestant Boys,
 Here's Millions of Joys,
And Triumph now bro . . . . ught from the Ocean ;
 For the *French* Mighty Fleet,
 Now is Shatter'd and Beat,
And Destruction, Destruction, Boys, will be their portion.

Woodcut illustration of the battle of La Hogue, from a contemporary broadsheet.

year grant to Sarah, over which she took issue, and then demanded that Sarah should be dismissed from Anne's service. Anne refused point blank. Mary then completely lost her temper and an angry scene, eagerly overheard by the servants outside, took place. Less than two weeks later, and no less suddenly, Marlborough found himself deprived of all his offices by William and forbidden to go to Court. No reason was given at the time and it became the talk of London, but according to Burnet, William had 'very good reason' to suspect him of dealings with the Jacobites and that he was doing 'all he could to set on a faction in the army and nation against the Dutch and to lessen the King'.

Meanwhile, Sarah remained in Anne's household; but when, a week or so after Marlborough's fall, Anne took her to Whitehall, she was deliberately flouting established etiquette which ruled that no wife of a disgraced officer should ever appear at Court. The next day Anne received a highly critical letter from her sister, saying bluntly, 'it is very unfit Lady Marlborough should stay with you'. Anne replied: 'You must needs be sensible enough of the kindness I have for my Lady Marlborough to know that a command from you to part with her must be the greatest mortification in the world to me, and indeed of such a nature as I might well have hoped your kindness to me would have always prevent.'

Rather than live at Whitehall without Sarah, Anne withdrew from the Cockpit to Syon House, lent to her by the Duke of Somerset. But the hostility continued, and indeed reached new peaks of spitefulness. William, who now 'entered the quarrels of women as if he had been one of them', tried to persuade Somerset to withdraw his hospitality; Anne's guards were removed from her (with the result that on one occasion she was robbed by highwaymen); the text of the sermon was no longer placed in her pew when she attended St James's Chapel; and later, when she and George made a visit to Bath, special instructions were sent to the Mayor, ordering him to ignore them. In April, the last occasion on which Mary and Anne were to meet ended in another scene. Anne had recently given birth to a son who lived only a few minutes and she was still in bed 'white as the sheets'. But Mary, far from showing sympathy, declared that she had made the first gesture by her visit and now she expected Sarah to be dismissed.

The quarrel between Anne and her sovereigns was heightened by the gathering political crisis which dominated the spring of 1692. For while his daughters were squabbling in London, in France James had at last persuaded Louis to back him in a full-scale invasion, not just of Ireland as in 1690, but of England itself. English spies reported that a fleet had assembled near Cherbourg and was only waiting for the wind to veer to the west before it sailed, and that James had set out from Paris to join it, full of hope and with summonses to a new Privy Council prepared in anticipation of his restoration. In England, while defences were quickly put in hand all along the coast, William was haunted by the possibility of Jacobite defections – even the Admiral of the Fleet, Lord Russell, was supposed to be unreliable. He need not have worried. The battle fought at sea in June off Cape La Hogue turned out to be a resounding victory for England. As Evelyn joyfully recorded, 'after all our apprehensions of being invaded and doubts of our success at sea, it pleased God to give us a great naval victory, to the utter ruin of the French Fleet, their Admiral and all their best men-of-war, transports, ships, etc'. James never even got as far as embarking,

81

but watched the action from the shore and tactlessly offended his French hosts by exclaiming admiringly, 'Ah none but my English seamen could do so brave an action!' When the battle was over, though, his enthusiasm vanished and he was bitterly disappointed: 'I entreat you,' he wrote to Louis, 'to interest yourself no more for a prince so unfortunate, but permit me to withdraw with my family, to some corner of the world where I may cease to be an interruption to your majesty's usual course of prosperity and glory.' There was good reason to prepare for Louis's displeasure, for La Hogue was a crucial defeat for him, as well as for his unfortunate protégé. France's pretensions to supremacy at sea were shattered, as it proved, not just for the rest of William's reign, but Anne's too. England was not only made safe from invasion, but the way was paved for the great European campaigns fought by Marlborough against the French in the years to come.

But while victory was being won in the Channel, Marlborough was locked up in the Tower of London, accused of plotting against William. A man called Young, one of those professional scoundrels and exposers of plots who proliferated in the seventeenth century, had obtained a specimen of his signature from a correspondence about the character of a servant; and from this and various other documents he had forged a 'bond of association' between various prominent Englishmen to kill or capture the King and to restore James to the throne. Young then ordered a confederate to hide this document in a flowerpot in the house of the unsuspecting Bishop of Rochester, and went off to inform the Cabinet of its existence. 'A dreadful plot broke out,' wrote Sarah, 'which was said to have been hid somewhere, I don't know where, in a flower pot.' The Bishop's establishment was searched but, ludicrously, the document was not found – for the flowerpot in question, near the servants' quarters, was overlooked. But even without it, a warrant was issued for Marlborough's arrest on the sole strength of Young's testimony – a witness whose most striking qualification was, according to Sarah, that despite his prison record he had not yet had his ears cut off.

With Marlborough a prisoner and while the invasion scare was still moving to its height, Sarah received a string of sympathetic letters from Anne at Syon. Sarah herself was, not unnaturally, looking for ways to ease the deteriorating situation, and suggested to Anne that it might, after all, be as well if she left her household, if only temporarily. The protest was immediate: 'I hope in Christ you will never think more of leaving me, for I would be sacrificed to do you the least service, and nothing but death can ever make me part with you. For if it be possible I am every day more and more yours.' Sarah, however, persisted and told Anne to consult George. But again the answer was adamant:

> Can you think either of us so wretched that for the sake of twenty thousand pounds and to be tormented from morning to night with flattering knaves and fools we would forsake those we have such obligations to, and that we are certain we are the occasion of all their misfortunes? ... No, my dear Mrs Freeman, never believe your faithful Mrs Morley will ever submit. She can wait with patience for a sunshine day, and if she does not live to see it, yet she hopes England will flourish again.

And so the feud was allowed to rumble on, with feeling running high on all sides. Even when Marlborough was released from the Tower later in the summer, he was not returned to his offices and he remained isolated from the Court.

On occasions William and Mary would show interest in Gloucester and announcements appeared in the *Gazette* of their presents to him – on one occasion a box of ivory tools worth £25. When he was sick, which was frequently, a Bedchamber woman would be sent to inquire after him, but 'whoever was sent used to come without any ceremony into the room where the Princess herself was, and passing by her as she stood or sat, without taking more notice of her than if she were a rocker, go directly up to the Duke and make their speech to him, or to the nurse, as he lay in her lap'. To Sarah it seemed studied insolence.

The deadlock was broken only by the sudden and quite unexpected death of the Queen who, in the winter of 1694, fell victim to an epidemic of smallpox. Anne wrote asking to be allowed to come to the bedside, but was refused on the grounds that it was necessary to keep the Queen as quiet as possible if there were to be any chance of recovery. But, after remaining unconscious for more than a week, Mary died on 28 December, aged only thirty-two, leaving William, for all his neglect of her while she lived, devastated by grief.

Anne, full of remorse, mourned her sincerely, though her own prospects were transformed by her sister's death. Mary, with her high spirits and vitality had been expected to outlive Anne, whose health deteriorated with every pregnancy. Now with only William's shaky life between her and the throne, she and the Marlboroughs could look forward more certainly to the dawning of their 'sunshine day'. And it meant, too, that William could no longer afford to keep Anne an exile from Court. In the New Year a formal reconciliation took place at Kensington Palace, where Anne, carried in her chair, was embraced tearfully by the King. Anne's guards were restored, and Syon House was once more thronged with visitors, who laughed uneasily at Lord Carnarvon's gauche remark, 'I hope that Your Highness will remember that I came to see you, when none of this company did.' Anne's changed fortunes reflected on Marlborough too, and at the end of March he was once more received by William. When he was again accused of being involved in a Jacobite conspiracy, William ignored the charge completely.

For the next few years Anne's life followed a more tranquil course. William invited her to live at St James's and she once more played her part at Court, though under William's dour régime it was all very different from the rollicking world of Charles II. That world, gaily centred on the effervescent round of balls and masques at Whitehall, was about to vanish in a more literal way as well. In the New Year of 1698 a Dutch laundress accidentally set some clothes alight while drying them and started a fire in which the Palace burned until it was gutted. Plans were made to rebuild it, but the work was never started and Whitehall remained a blackened ruin until most of it was pulled down in the middle of the eighteenth century.

To Anne the fire snapped the last link with her youth. By now, though only in her thirties, she was a middle-aged woman, stout and often in ill-health. Her dismal catalogue of pregnancies was ending, for whereas between 1696 and 1700 she had five miscarriages, after 1700, when she was thirty-five, she never became pregnant again. In 1698 came the first mention of gout and in October she described herself to Sarah as 'a perfect cripple'. Now lack of exercise in turn finished off the ruin of her figure. And, for the pain, there was no relief except

ABOVE James II's children by his second marriage: James Francis Edward Stuart, with his sister Louisa Maria, who was born in exile in 1692. This double portrait was painted by Largillière in 1695.

William, Duke of
Gloucester, Anne's only
child to survive infancy,
and the heir to the English
throne. Godfrey Kneller
painted this portrait of
him in 1699 when the
Duke was ten.

laudanum and, perhaps, the rumoured secret brandy-drinking,
though this was loyally denied by Sarah.

Gloucester was probably the subject that occupied most of
her thoughts during this period. He was growing up into a
precocious boy who shared his uncle's military interests, and
from the time he was eight, the little Prince commanded an
'army' of about twenty Kensington youths, whom he eagerly
drilled and trained in the gardens of Campden House. But his
vigour was impaired by inexplicable fits of giddiness for which
the doctors could do nothing. Anne sensibly wanted him to
lead as quiet a life as possible but the servants spoiled him
atrociously, he was also inevitably a public figure. Not only

85

were his ailments, his presents and journeyings all diligently chronicled in the *Gazette*, and were sometimes the subject of minutes at Committee meetings of the Privy Council, but every detail of his development and upbringing was widely discussed.

When Gloucester was nine, a separate household was formed for him, and it was another sign of Marlborough's slowly rising fortunes that William appointed him Governor. But it was not a post he was to enjoy for long. Gloucester's eleventh birthday, in July 1700, was celebrated at Windsor with the splendour appropriate for a future King, and after a display of fireworks followed by a great banquet in the Castle, the excited boy retired to bed exhausted. The next day, a Friday, he woke with a fever and nausea and complained of a sore throat. The hastily-summoned physicians decided they should bleed him in order to lower the fever which, for a few hours, seemed to slacken its hold on the Prince, but only to return more violently than ever in the evening. As his condition deteriorated, Radcliffe, the most eminent doctor of the day, was sent for, but when he heard of the blood-letting he declared to the anxious physicians, 'Then you have destroyed him and you may finish him for I will not prescribe.'

Whether or not it was the bleeding that fatally weakened him, Gloucester was indeed dying. He lived for another four days, constantly delirious, shouting and tossing in his bed, while Anne sat beside him, praying and hoping for a miracle that would save him. But on the following Monday, just before midnight, he died. Anne's composure in face of this terrible blow awed those around her. She did not weep and Prince George could only marvel at the 'pious fortitude of his beloved Princess'. But beneath the calm she was stunned with grief and Gloucester's death, which sealed the tragedy of her motherhood, turned Anne into a sad woman, facing the future with little enthusiasm.

She continued to hope for some years that she would become pregnant – it would have been for the eighteenth time – but only a sublime optimist could have believed that there was any chance of her bearing another child. To Parliament Gloucester's death meant the end of the Protestant Stuart line, and they felt it necessary to provide for the succession after Anne's

The proclamation of the accession of Anne to the throne in 1701. The Queen still laid claim to the Crown of France, as did all British monarchs until 1801.

death. So in 1701 the Act of Settlement was passed, laying down that if Anne died with no children, the Crown should pass from her to her Hanoverian cousins, the descendants of James 1's daughter, and the nearest Protestant members of the royal family. It was said that more than fifty-two Catholic members with a better claim were passed over, and it was clear that if the Hanoverians ever did inherit the throne they, even more than William, would owe their title to Parliament.

The eighteenth century quickly brought two other deaths in the royal family. From France in September Anne received the news of her father's death. His widow, Mary of Modena, wrote to tell her that a few days before he died, James had said 'he forgave you all that is past from the bottom of his heart and prayed to God to do so too'. But in James's eyes it was his son, not Anne, who should be ruler of England after his death, and as well as forgiveness for the wrongs to himself, Mary of Modena told Anne, 'he gave you his last blessing and prayed to God to convert your heart and confirm you in the resolution of repairing to his son the wrongs done to himself'. Anne did not reply to the letter, but in the years that followed there were Jacobite stories, almost certainly false, that shortly before James's death Anne had promised him that she would somehow make reparations to his son – not by renouncing the Crown herself, but by leaving it to him after her own death. In France, even before James's death, Louis had promised to recognise his son as the rightful King of England.

In England William outlived his father-in-law by less than six months. In February 1702, as he was riding near Hampton Court, his horse stumbled on a mole-hill and he fell, breaking his collar-bone. In itself it was a minor injury, but in his frail body it was the last he could sustain. By the night of 8 March he was reported to be nearing his end.

At St James's the stout middle-aged sister-in-law, for whom he had displayed such open contempt, and whom he now curtly refused to allow at his bedside, waited up for news throughout the night. As the sun rose it was Mulgrave, now Marquess of Normanby, the suitor of her youth, who was admitted to her presence and, when she remarked to him on the fineness of the weather, replied, 'Your Majesty must allow me to declare that it is the most glorious day I ever saw.'

87

FACIT
CONIUNCTIO
TUTOS.

4
'Entirely
English'
1702-4

WITHIN AN HOUR of William's death, Londoners were woken by the tolling of their church bells and by the shouts of the black-capped heralds as they solemnly trudged the streets: 'The King is dead! Long live the Queen!' Inside St James's Palace, Anne was already facing her first duties of sovereignty, and only a few hours after her accession she was seated on the dais in the Presence Chamber, with the crimson canopy of State above her head, preparing to read her first speech to the hastily-assembled Privy Council. There had been no time to change, but during her long night vigil she had in any case been wearing the deepest mourning for Gloucester and for James, and now the grave dignity of her manner combined with her clear musical voice, trained by Mrs Barry for the Whitehall masques of nearly a quarter of a century before, made a favourable impression on her curious audience. Lord Dartmouth voiced the general approval when he declared that 'it was a real pleasure to hear her though she had a bashfulness that made it very uneasy to herself to say much in public'.

It was not just among the ruling circles that people hastened to welcome the new reign. National mourning for William was so brief and perfunctory as to be almost indecent, underlining the general relief at once more having a sovereign who was wholly English. For Anne was English in a way that set her apart not just from William but from all English monarchs since the death of Queen Elizabeth I almost exactly a hundred years before. Her Stuart predecessors had been in some way divided from their subjects. James I had been a Scotsman, Charles I had gone to war against half his kingdom, and Anne's uncle and father, Charles II and James II, had both allowed their French and Catholic leanings to stand between them and the wishes and prejudices of their subjects. But Anne, for all the mixture of Italian, French, Scottish and Danish blood in her veins, was completely in tune with the solid mass of her English subjects. She echoed their dislike of France, their suspicion of all things Catholic, and in both the crisis of 1688 and the subsequent disenchantment with William, Anne had reflected the feelings of the kingdom against her own family. Perhaps she owed more to her Hyde forebears than she did to her Stuart ancestors, for even her personal characteristics – her greed, her gout, her gambling – were reassuringly ordinary;

Queen Anne in her State Coach in procession to Parliament. The coach, accompanied by an escort of Household Cavalry, walking footmen and Yeomen of the Guard is shown approaching the Old House Guards: painting attributed to Alexander van Gaelen.

and her stolid appearance, too – mid-brown hair, rather florid complexion and portly figure – could be counted an asset.

Anne was, therefore, by nature and inclination, a mirror and a mouthpiece for the middle-of-the-road English attitudes. She was, undoubtedly, a very limited woman; but her limitations strengthened her convictions, and from the beginning she approached her new office with a determination to do her duty. In the years to come it was her tireless conscience, and her unalterable desire to do everything correctly, that forced her to drag herself to endless Council meetings, to cope with the piles of State papers, and to deal with the more direct demands of her ordinary subjects – their petitions and the long queues of the sick hoping to be touched for the Queen's Evil. Though Anne would be mocked, and her abilities questioned, of her honest devotion to her country there was never any doubt; and she never forfeited the strong bond of affection and goodwill which existed between her and her subjects.

Three days after her accession, when Anne rode in state to address her first Parliament, this theme of a patriot queen was cleverly exploited. Her dress seemed to be modelled from a portrait of Elizabeth I, and as she slowly walked up to the throne, there was a buzz of approval. Her robe was of red velvet lined with ermine and trimmed with gold; round her neck hung a thick gold chain bearing the badge of St George; and on her head her red velvet cap was surmounted by the Crown of

England. Her message matched the occasion: 'As I know my heart to be entirely English,' she declared, 'I can very sincerely assure you that there is not one thing you can expect or desire of me which I shall not be ready to do for the happiness or prosperity of England. ...' Her audience was enchanted and rushed to praise her looks, her words and her voice. Speaker Onslow declared he had never seen the members so moved, and added, 'it was a sort of charm'.

Anne certainly made a welcome change from the asthmatic Dutchman with the rasping voice, but for all that the new reign did not inaugurate any departure from William's policies. England in 1702 was once more on the verge of war with France and there was no question of drawing back. Within eight hours of her accession Anne had written to the Dutch States-General assuring them that the death of 'our very dear Brother of Glorious Memory' would make no difference to England's commitments overseas. William's Grand Alliance between Holland, England and the Emperor would still be the basis of her policy and Anne was ready to support 'all measures which it will be necessary to take in preserving the liberty of Europe and reducing the power of France to its just limits'.

Here – at last – was Marlborough's chance and there was little doubt about the role he was destined to play. As Sarah's husband and her own confidant, where else was Anne to turn? Marlborough himself was prepared; and had, indeed, spent the last months of the old reign knitting together the Alliance which would win his battles and his immortality in the new. The tension which disfigured William's relations with John Churchill had evaporated with the growing threat of war. Now in his fifties, Marlborough had at last been given the scope and recognition which was his due. Appointments, influence and honours were no longer withheld, and at the beginning of the new century he found himself enjoying the impressive title of Ambassador Extraordinary and Plenipotentiary for negotiations with the Empire, the States-General and other Emissaries at The Hague; and he became, in addition, the Commander-in-Chief of all the British forces in the Netherlands.

Not surprisingly England's allies counted him the coming man. The States-General put at his disposal the magnificent Mauritshuis, where Charles II had feasted on the eve of his

93

restoration, and there, with unfailing tact, sagacity and charm (even his own individual brand of bad French delighted all he met), Marlborough presided over an endless series of meetings with the princes, diplomats and envoys of other countries. It was an invaluable experience. Perhaps William, in the knowledge that he was dying, had deliberately trained Marlborough to carry on his life's work; but here the pupil was abler than his master, for Marlborough, with his easy affability and exhaustive patience, quickly proved himself a better diplomat than the King. And one mistake of William's Marlborough studiously avoided: never in his whole career did he neglect the susceptibilities of the House of Commons. The Duke, dedicated as he was to the Alliance he was building, would make no commitment of English troops abroad without consent from Parliament at home.

But if abroad Anne's succession brought no change in England's policies, at home the personal wishes of the new Queen were making their impact. After a lifetime spent at Court, when it came to the business of distributing office and favours to her friends and supporters she felt more confident of what she was about, and all who had shared with her the troubles of past reigns could now expect their reward.

Prince George was the first to be singled out and, for a time, it seemed as if his position would cause trouble. For Anne proposed to make him not only King Consort in England but, if the Dutch could be persuaded to agree, Stadtholder in the Netherlands as well. Nobody else, in either England or the Netherlands, shared her enthusiasm, but it was only after much tactful dissuasion that she gave up the idea. Even then it was only to appoint him Generalissimo of all her forces and Lord High Admiral of the Fleet, which was scarcely more acceptable. By this time bovine George had long since cast aside all ambitions and energy – it was reported that he loved only 'his news, his bottle, and the Queen'.

Even Marlborough found his powers momentarily eclipsed by Anne's ambitions for George, for William's death meant that there was a vacancy not just at the head of England's forces, but at the head of all the armies of the Alliance, and Anne felt it would be a splendid compensation for all George's rebuffs under William, if he were now appointed supreme allied

OPPOSITE Equestrian portrait of John Churchill, 1st Duke of Marlborough, at the height of his fame, painted by Godfrey Kneller, c. 1706.

commander. The idea, to anyone but her, was patently absurd and the Dutch would never have tolerated it for a moment; yet Marlborough found himself entrusted with the delicate task of being George's advocate at The Hague for the very position he coveted himself. It is an impressive testimony to his diplomatic skills that he managed to let Anne down without offending her, George, the Dutch, or anyone else.

Not that Marlborough had much to complain of on his own account. Within a week Anne had appointed him Captain-General of her armies both at home and abroad and, as well, had granted him two favours specifically withheld by William – the Garter and the lucrative post of Master-General of the Ordnance. Marlborough's days of financial insecurity were over: within a year or two of Anne's accession, the income from his various positions amounted to some £60,000 a year, and by the time he died he was a millionaire.

As for Sarah, what arrangement could be more satisfactory than to have the ear of the Queen at home while her husband defended England's interests abroad? It was natural that, when Anne formed her household, Mrs Freeman should also be showered with positions and favours, and Sarah happily totted up the extra money they brought her. She was made Groom of the Stole, Keeper of the Privy Purse and Mistress of the Robes, which meant an annual income, quite apart from Marlborough's, of at least £5,600, not to mention the £1,000 a year received by her two elder daughters, Harriet and Anne, as ladies of the Bedchamber.

Sarah, characteristically, did not regard her offices as mere sinecures, and with determined energy applied her thrifty instincts to the task of putting in order the Privy Purse and administering Anne's wardrobe. Accustomed to the casual inefficiency with which most Court office holders performed their duties, Anne may well have been taken aback by Sarah's zeal. The Queen, Sarah decided, should appear without ostentation and Anne's meek objections that she was being dressed too poorly were firmly quashed. It would be ridiculous, Sarah insisted, for a woman of Anne's age and shape to deck herself out in all manner of finery. She already had 'everything handsome and proper for her' and, in any case, Anne's gout meant she could not bear the weight of heavy materials about her limbs. Even for State occasions there was to be no extravagance. Jewels could be hired and robes quite well refurbished. In her meticulously kept account book, which is still at Blenheim, occur such entries as 'a Parliament robe of crimson genoa lined with white mantua and with the old ermine cleaned and put in again'. It could hardly have been more of a contrast with the stupendous extravagance of Louis XIV's Versailles, where the King never wore the same shoes more than once, and could have fitted out a battalion with the money he spent on jewels. Something of Anne's reactions to this strict régime emerges from her letters to Sarah : 'I had in mind to be fine too,' she once confessed, 'and in order to be so I intended to have two diamond buttons and loops on each sleeve.' But usually she gave way meekly, rather than face an argument which Sarah would win with her characteristic retort, 'Lord Madam! But it must be so!'

'I had in mind to be fine too'

Even Sarah did, however, relax her rules for the coronation, which took place on 23 April – St George's Day – and was a national holiday. On this day, at least, there could be no complaints about Anne's lack of finery, and an enraptured eye-witness wrote down a precise description. Her dress was of crimson velvet with an under-robe of 'gold tissue, very rich embroidery of jewels about it, her petticoat the same gold tissue with gold and silver lace between rows of diamonds embroidered, her linen fine ... her head as well dressed with diamonds that brilled and flared'. Sarah's accounts show an unusually lavish outlay of £10.15s. for 'dressing Her Majesty's head' and a further £12 for supplying 'a head of hair with long locks and puffs' – so it seems Anne wore a wig for the occasion.

It was a cruel blow to her that, weighted down by all this magnificence, she also happened to be suffering from a severe attack of gout, and therefore gained the dubious distinction of being the only English monarch who had to be carried to her coronation. And so it was that Anne, carried by the Yeomen of the Guard in an open sedan chair with a low back, over which her six-yard train could pass to her ladies behind, arrived in Westminster Abbey shortly after eleven o'clock. The ceremony took over five hours, and for a gouty invalid must have been an exhausting ordeal. The Archbishop of York, whom Anne preferred as being more High Church than Canterbury, preached the sermon, and then she was finally crowned late in

97

The installation of the
Knights of the Garter by
Queen Anne at Windsor in
1713; canvas by P. Angelis.

98

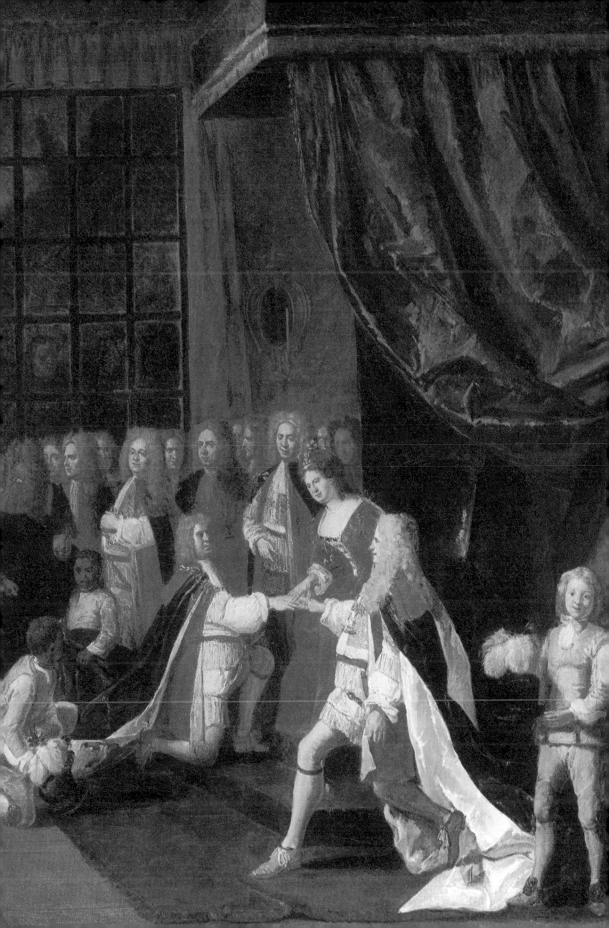

HET
GESCHIL,
Tuſſchen de
Franſche Haan, en *Lombaardſche*
Hennen,
Beſlegt door *Jupiter*.

Volgens de *Romeinſe Copy*.

Political satire of 1700.
Louis XIV, represented by
the French cock, claims
power over Lombardy.
The hens complain to
Jupiter, who orders the
eagle – William III – to
attack the cock and
save them.

the afternoon by the Archbishop of Canterbury, who also
expressed the rather tactless hope that she would 'leave a
numerous posterity to rule these kingdoms'. It all passed without a hitch, though it must have been an anxious moment when
Anne rose from her chair and staggered uncertainly to the altar
to be anointed.

Two weeks later, on 4 May, England declared war against
France. 'It means I'm growing old when ladies declare war on
me,' joked Louis when he was told. But his levity was mis-
placed. Europe was on the verge of a conflict of unprecedented

100

scale that would last for the next twelve years and impoverish his kingdom. In one sense this was the culminating phase in the long struggle to check Louis's ambitions that had dominated Europe for almost half a century. Yet this time the stakes were larger than they had ever been before, for the issue over which England and the rest of the Grand Alliance were preparing to go to war was the fate of the vast Spanish Empire, both in Europe itself and overseas. The late King of Spain, another Charles II, had been a childless invalid with no direct heir, and the two main claimants to succeed him were Philip of Anjou, a grandson of Louis XIV, and the Habsburg Archduke Charles, whose families had already been rivals for centuries and each of whom was quite unacceptable to the other. But when Charles II finally died in November 1700, concerned not with the future of European peace but with the unity of his own empire, in his will he had left the whole inheritance to the French claimant, Philip.

To be fair to Louis, he was placed in an impossible position. His days of war-mongering were over and he was growing old and reluctant to lead his impoverished country into another full-scale European conflict. He had, even before the Spanish King's death, co-operated with William in trying to devise a peaceful solution to the problem, and in 1699 had signed a Partition Treaty with him agreeing to a division of Spanish lands between the French and Austrian claimants. But both Spain and Austria had refused to accept the treaty or the principle of partition on which it was based, and their refusal made it quite unworkable even if Louis had tried to stick by it. And now in Charles's will Louis's grandson was offered everything, but with a proviso saying that Louis should back his claim. If he did not, then Philip would get nothing and the whole dazzling prize would pass to the Austrian Archduke Charles. Not surprisingly Louis despatched his grandson with French troops to Madrid to be crowned Philip V of Spain. He then abandoned all pretence of moderation and, having already antagonised England by his recognition of the Pretender, sent another French force into the Spanish Netherlands and seized the fortresses legally garrisoned by the Dutch to protect their western frontiers.

It was aggression that sprang from over-confidence, for France could not believe that England without William would fight wholeheartedly in Europe. Anne was hardly a warlike figure, and they felt no reason to fear the Earl of Marlborough. Nor was this attitude unduly arrogant, for Marlborough's fighting record was so far not an outstanding one. His chief qualification in the eyes of the French was that he had served under the great Turenne, but that was as a junior officer over twenty years before. Since then they had fought him in Ireland and in Flanders, but there was nothing to indicate that he would prove as formidable a foe as William: today French schoolchildren are still taught a song, 'Marlbrouk s'en va t'en guerre', but in 1702, most Frenchmen had never even heard of him.

Louis drew comfort, too, from the fact that Anne was known to favour the Tories. Few generalisations about political parties in Anne's reign stand up to close inspection, but there was a definite and persistent distinction between the Whig and Tory attitudes towards the war. It was the Tories who were the more insular, and who supported the Alliance with less enthusiasm. They were willing enough to support a war at sea, perhaps even in the first flush of enthusiasm to try to drive Philip of Anjou off the throne of Spain, but the prospect of re-enacting William's costly and unspectacular campaigns in Flanders they eyed with suspicion. To many a Tory squire all foreigners were more or less alike: the Dutch were as bad as the French, and for England to pour more men and money into this dreary corner of north-eastern Europe would be both an unnecessary involvement in Continental affairs which were best left to the Continentals, and, with the land tax providing the main source of funds for the war, an unwelcome drain on their purses.

But in 1702, with Englishmen smarting from Louis's recognition of the Pretender, even Tory opposition to the war was muted, and Anne was not the only person who failed to see any contradiction between her desire to support Marlborough and the war on the one hand, and her sympathy with the Tory position at home on the other. The Tories had been confused by the 1688 Revolution, which shattered their cherished belief in the legitimate succession: yet they remained the most ardent supporters of a ruling monarchy and, as the party that defended the privileges of the Church of England, were now particularly delighted at the accession of an Anglican monarch after first a Catholic and then a Calvinist. As for the Whigs, Sarah was

The song 'Marlbrouk s'en va t'en guerre', sung by French children in the first decade of the eighteenth century, is reproduced on a ballad-sheet reporting the news of the Duke's death in 1722.

MORT ET CONVOI
DE L'INVINCIBLE MALBOROUGH.

TOMBEAU.

Malborough s'en va-t-en guerre ; Mironton mironton mirontaine ; Malborough s'en va-t-en guerre, ne sait quand reviendra.

Ne sait quand reviendra, ne sait quand reviendra : il reviendra à Pâques, mironton mironton mirontaine : il reviendra à Pâques ou à la Trinité.

La Trinité se passe, mironton etc. Malborough ne revient pas.

Madame à sa tour monte mironton etc. si haut qu'elle peut monter.

Elle voit venir son Page, mironton etc. de noir tout habillé.

Beau page, ah! mon beau page, mironton etc. quelle

nouvelle apportez.

Aux nouvelles que j'apporte, mironton etc. vos beaux yeux vont pleurer.

Quittez vos habits roses, mironton etc. et vos satins brochés.

Monsieur d'Malborough est mort, mironton, etc. est mort et enterré.

J'ai vu porter en

terre, mironton etc. par quatre officiers.

L'un portait sa Cuirasse, mironton etc. et l'autre son Bouclier.

L'un portait son grand Sabre, mironton etc. et l'autre rien ne porta.

A l'entour de sa tombe mironton etc. Romarins l'on plata.

Sur la plus haute branche, mironton etc. le Rossignol chanta.

On vit voler son ame, mironton etc. au travers des lauriers.

Chacun mit ventre à terre, mironton etc. et puis se releva.

Pour chanter les victoires, mironton

etc. que Malborough remporta.

La cérémonie faite, mironton etc. chacun s'en fut coucher.

Les uns avec leurs femmes, miron. etc. et les autres tous seuls.

Ce n'est pas qu'il en manque, miron. etc. car j'en connais beaucoup.

Des blondes et puis des brunes, mironton etc. et des chataignes aussi.

J'en en dis pas davantage, mironton etc. car en voilà assez.

FIN.

MONTBÉLIARD,
de l'Imprimerie de Deckherr.

putting it too strongly when she said that Anne regarded them 'as not only Republicans who hated the very shadow of royal authority, but implacable enemies of the Church of England'; but she certainly regarded them with great suspicion. Whig support of Dissenters and their irreverent attitude to the throne were quite enough to have set her firmly against them.

This did not mean that Anne wanted her first ministry to be composed purely of Tories, for the doctrine that government offices should be filled by members of the ruling party had not yet evolved. It was still considered to be a vital part of the Queen's prerogatives that she should make all the government appointments herself, and Anne shared the view of all her predecessors that she should be perfectly free in making this choice, and that the allegiances of her ministers should be to the Crown, and not to any 'party or faction'.

Nevertheless, Anne's first ministry was, predictably, composed mainly of Tories. 'My Lord Normanby' (soon after Duke of Buckingham), Sarah noted, 'the Earls of Jersey and Nottingham, Sir Edward Seymour, with many other High Fliers were brought into Place.' It was reported that when Anne had removed the Whig Lord Wharton's staff of office as Comptroller of the household, and had handed it in his presence to his worst Tory enemy, Edward Seymour, she had done so with visible pleasure. The most important office of Lord Treasurer was given, at Marlborough's request, to his friend Godolphin – not that Anne needed much persuading. Sydney Godolphin had been a familiar figure at Whitehall since her childhood. A member of a Royalist family from Cornwall, he had come to make his way at the Court of Charles II soon after the Restoration, and had quickly proved himself an effective and tactful royal servant, described by the King as 'never in the way and never out of it'. He had married in secret Margaret Blagge, one of the maids-of-honour at Court who used to act with Anne and Sarah in the Whitehall masques, but less than a year after the wedding she had died in childbirth, leaving Godolphin one baby son, Francis. After this brief taste of an exceptionally happy marriage, Godolphin remained a widower for the rest of his live, devoting himself to his work at the Treasury and to his one hobby – horse-racing. He was one of the very few men for whom Sarah had a great respect:

Sydney, 1st Earl of Godolphin, holding his white wand of office as Lord Treasurer. Portrait by Godfrey Kneller, *c.* 1705.

He was a man of few words, but of a remarkable thoughtfulness and sedateness of temper; of great application to business ... of wonderful frugality in the public concerns but of no great carefulness about his own. He affected being useful without popularity ; and the inconsiderable sum of money ... which he left at his death showed that he had been indeed the nation's treasurer and not his own.

In 1702 Godolphin, like Marlborough, could be described as a 'Tory without zeal', though both their appointments differed from the general Tory scramble for office, in that both were first and foremost servants of the Crown, rather than adherents to a label. Godolphin was a royal minister of the old school. His task, as he saw it, was to manage the government, and in Parliament he would look for support for his measures from wherever it was forthcoming. The extremes of both parties

Robert Harley, 1st Earl of Oxford and Mortimer, who became Lord Treasurer in 1711: portrait by Godfrey Kneller, 1714.

served mostly to cause factions and disputes, and too often to obstruct government business. It was the duty of any responsible administration to distribute its favours to secure the most effective results in terms of amenable votes, and to look to men of the centre who, like himself, wore their party allegiances lightly.

Sarah had quite a different opinion of the third and junior member of the Marlborough-Godolphin partnership and, as usual, she did not mince her words. Robert Harley was to her

> ... a cunning and a dark man, of too small abilities to do much good, but with all the qualities requisite to do mischief and to bring on the ruin and destruction of a nation. This mischievousness and darkness of his soul was written in his countenance and plainly legible in a very odd look, disagreeable to everybody at first sight. ... He had long accustomed himself so much to dissemble his real intentions and to use the ambiguous and obscure way of speaking that he could hardly ever be understood when he really designed it, or be believed when he never so much desired it.

Yet Harley, for all his secrecy and cunning, had genuine abilities that Sarah totally missed. While both Marlborough and

Godolphin were too sensitive and thin-skinned to relish the rough battles of politics, Harley, less able as a financier and an administrator, possessed an almost uncanny ability to manage the House of Commons that was invaluable ; and it was a combination of Marlborough abroad and Godolphin and Harley at home that handled the government during the first years of the reign.

In May, Anne dismissed William's old Parliament with a firm declaration about her devotion to the Church of England and all who supported it and, though the subsequent General Election was fiercely fought, no one was greatly surprised when this firm expression of the Crown's electoral sympathies contributed to the return of a House of Commons that was distinctly Tory in complexion. But the Whigs were strong in the House of Lords, and, with the Tories in a belligerent mood against the Whigs if not the French, Anne soon had cause to feel that Parliament was a quarrelsome, unco-operative body.

One of the first Parliamentary crises of the reign involved her consort, George – the fight over the Tories' Occasional Conformity Bill, introduced in November 1702. This was devised to put a stop to the Dissenters' practice of qualifying for public office by taking communion in the Anglican Church once a year. It was bound to be hotly controversial, and the Whigs, with their dissenting sympathies, opposed it with vehemence. But Anne supported it as a measure which upheld the Church of England, despite the fact that George was an 'occasional conformist' himself, worshipping regularly in a private Lutheran chapel, but qualifying for his State offices by taking Anglican communion at intervals. Incongruously, therefore, he was sent off to vote for the bill in the Lords, and as he dutifully lumbered towards the Tory lobby he was reported to have whispered to one of the Whig leaders, 'My heart is vid you.' Despite George's vote, the bill foundered in the Lords, and had to be shelved for the time being ; but it had given a taste of the tense party battles to come.

For Anne these battles were fought closer to home, as Sarah, alone of the old circle at the Cockpit, was a Whig ; and she was as thorough in this as she was in everything else. She did not modify her feelings to please her royal mistress, but instead set out to convert her. To Sarah all Tories were dangerously feeble in their support of the war and she had no sympathy at all with their doctrines at home. Tory zeal in support of the Church she contemptuously condemned as so much empty cant: 'For my own part, the word Church had never any charm for me in the mouths of those who made the most noise with it; for I could not perceive that they gave any other distinguishing proof of their Regard for the thing than a frequent use of the Word, like a spell to enchant weak minds.' As for their loyalty to the Crown, she warned Anne bluntly that this might change into Jacobitism if the opportunity arose.

The trouble was that Sarah never knew when to stop. Anne might want to chat about her plans for the royal gardens, or share the latest snippet of town gossip, 'twitell twatell' she called it herself, but Sarah seized every opportunity to nag her about the Whigs. Not that she made much progress, for Anne's mind was firmly made up: 'I cannot help being extremely concerned you are so partial to the Whigs,' she wrote on one occasion, 'because I would not have you and your poor un-fortunate faithful Morley differ in opinion in the least thing.' But she stuck firmly to her views and declared staunchly, '... and upon my word, my dear Mrs Freeman, you are mightily mistaken in your notion of a true Whig; for the character you give of them does not in the least belong to them but to the Church'.

Sarah was tactless in other ways too. While the other ladies in attendance had subtly altered their manner in deference to a queen, Sarah carried on as before, at one moment arguing, at the next turning her back to talk to someone else. Yet Anne's affection seemed unquenchable, and continued to be expressed in very tangible ways. When Sarah's eldest daughter had married Francis Godolphin, Anne had given as a wedding present what she humbly termed 'a mite' of £10,000; and on the marriage of her god-daughter Anne to the new Earl of Sunderland, another magnificent royal gift was pressed on the young couple, and that despite the fact that Sunderland was a Whig. Sarah herself had always shown a particular fondness for the Lodge at Windsor, and so now, shortly after her corona-tion, Anne offered her the use of it for the rest of her life because 'everything that is of so much satisfaction as this poor place seems to be to you, I would give my dear Mrs Freeman for all her days which I pray God may be as many and as happy as this world can make you'.

Not surprisingly there were those who believed Sarah ruled the Queen, and nicknamed her the Vicereine, or Queen Sarah. She was, of course, regarded as an obvious stepping-stone to Anne's favour and was besieged by office-hunters. 'I began to be looked on as a person of consequence,' she reported in her *Conduct* 'without whose approbation at least neither places, nor pensions, nor honours were bestowed by the Crown.' But Anne was capable of making a distinction between their private relationship and her role as Queen, which Sarah rashly ignored. Personally Anne remained under her sway, longing to see her, jealous of other friendships, fretting anxiously in her absences, but Anne had an awesome concept of her royal office which she laboured devoutly to uphold, and which Sarah underestimated. If the Queen believed some of the Whigs to be truly wicked, then Sarah was merely wasting her breath in pushing their appointments to public office. As for Church appointments, Anne always insisted on making these herself, and when a friend wrote to Sarah asking her to exert her influence with the Queen over a clerical office, Sarah felt obliged to admit that she could be of no assistance and that her opinion carried no weight.

What Marlborough thought of Sarah's Whiggery is uncertain, but though he could not have approved it, he was a mild husband and shrank from crossing her. In any case he had other preoccupations – in particular to cement his Alliance and create from it a force capable of defeating the French. These were scarcely easy tasks, and were made less so by the Dutch who, though they had reluctantly given him command of their forces serving with the English, had also saddled him with the constant supervision of two Dutch deputies who were empowered to veto any action they considered inadvisable.

In the first summer of the war a French force withdrew from the Meuse Valley in disarray, after Marlborough had cut off their supply line. The retreat could have been turned into a rout, but the cautious Dutch deputies thought a battle unnecessarily rash. Marlborough took them to watch the enemy retreating 'in the greatest confusion and disorder imaginable' to prove his point, but it was a big disappointment, and he felt compelled to send trumpets to the French commander, Boufflers, and to his

'I had began to be looked on as a person of consequence'

109

Painted wooden figure, 6 ft high, which was used in recruiting campaigns for the British army in the early eighteenth century.

RIGHT Coloured engraving of the Battle of Blenheim, 13 August 1704.

Eighteenth-century painted battle-drum.

The Attack upon the Village of BLE... ...ere taken Twenty Eight Battallions & 9... ...dismounted Dragoons, being ÿ best T...

ch | *A Brigade of French Foot in y^e Center of*
s | y^e *Field of Battle near* BLENHEIM *cut*
. | *in Pieces being abandoned by their Horse.*

Prince EUGENE *of* SAVOY *attacking* y^e *Left Wing of* y^e *French*
Army at y^e *Battle of* BLENHEIM *commanded by* y^e *Elector*
of BAVARIA *and the Mareshall* MARSIN

own nephew, Berwick, to assure them with his compliments that it was not his fault he had not attacked. But even if Marlborough could not bring the French to battle, by the autumn he had a string of successful sieges to his name and the towns of Venloo, Stevensweert, Ruremonde and Liege had all fallen to his arms.

At first the war at sea had not fared so well. The English and Dutch Grand Fleets had made a disastrous attempt to seize Cadiz, but had redeemed themselves by then proceeding to capture the Spanish treasure fleet from the West Indies as it lay at anchor in Vigo Bay. There was certainly enough scope to draw happy comparisons between Queen Elizabeth and the Armada and Queen Anne and the new war. A formal thanksgiving service was held in Wren's nearly-completed St Paul's Cathedral, and as Anne drove to the City with Sarah and Anne Sunderland beside her, from the Tower there crashed out a repeated salvo of guns, and the streets were festooned with tapestries and banners.

BELOW Section of a First-Rate Ship of 1700. She carried armament of 100 guns and a crew of 850, and her best speed was 10 knots.

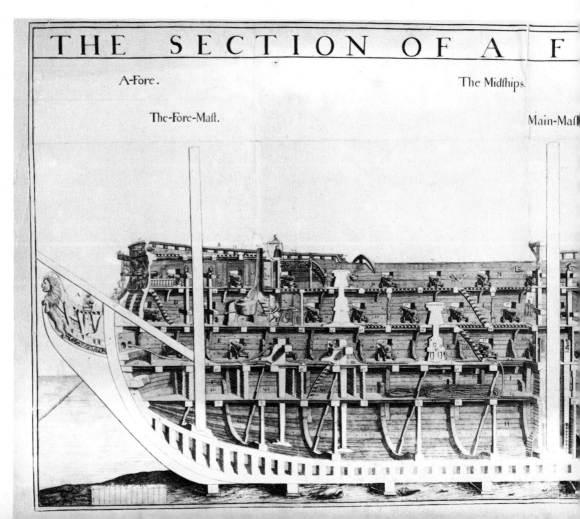

THE SECTION OF A F

A-Fore.

The Midships.

The-Fore-Maft.

Main-Maf

T RATE SHIP

By Capt Bos Phillips
second Engineer
of England

A-Bauſt.

Miſon-Maſt.

ABOVE A bird's-eye view of the breaking of the boom by the English and Dutch ships in Vigo Bay, 12 October 1702. The allied fleets, under the command of Sir George Rooke, broke through the boom behind which the Spanish treasure fleet, guarded by French warships, was sheltered in the harbour of Redondela. Painting by an unknown artist.

For Anne the most important thing was to find a suitable reward for her great general, and after much thought, she decided to bestow on him the highest rank it was within her power to give. Before the season's campaigning was over, she had written to Sarah, 'It is very uneasy to your poor unfortunate faithful Morley to think she has so very little in her power to show how truly sensible I am of all my Lord Marlborough's kindnesses. ... But since there is nothing else at this time, I hope you will give me leave, as soon as he comes, to make him a Duke.' Surprisingly, Sarah was at first unenthusiastic. Her feet were too firmly planted on the ground for her to be dazzled by empty titles, and Marlborough, she felt, had not yet acquired sufficient wealth to support such an exalted rank. Anne tried to remedy the point by persuading Parliament to grant the dukedom £5,000 a year in perpetuity, but when 'with inexpressible grief' they declined to co-operate, restricting the grant to Anne's lifetime, she once more offered to help herself. 'Would dear Mr and Mrs Freeman be so kind,' she wrote, 'as to accept two thousand pounds a year from the Privy Purse'; no one need ever know about it and so no one need ever be envious. Possibly in a moment of pique Sarah refused, and Marlborough became a Duke without immediately acquiring any additional income; but nine years later Sarah was to reclaim the amount Anne had offered them in full, plus arrears. It was a poor return for such generous treatment.

For the new Duke of Marlborough and his Duchess the year 1703 began tragically. Their only son, the Marquess of Blandford, was seventeen years old and studying at Cambridge. He was a promising boy 'of a comely beautiful form, affable temper, and excellent parts' who kept pestering his father to take him to the wars. His godfather was Godolphin, and in February young Blandford went from Cambridge to pay him a visit at Newmarket. Within a few days he was dead. An outbreak of smallpox was then scourging the town, and though Sarah rushed to his bedside and Anne despatched her own doctor, nothing could be done to save him. Sarah was demented with grief, shutting herself up at St Albans, refusing to see anyone, ignoring Anne's sympathy, and threatening never to go to Court again. When she finally came to London she avoided St James's and was said to have haunted the cloisters of West-

'I have lost what is so dear to me. It is fit for me to retire'

114

minster Abbey, clothed entirely in black. As for Marlborough, 'I have lost what is so dear to me, it is fit for me to retire and not toil and labour for I know not who.'

The military scene brought him no comfort. The successes of the previous year were not repeated. The Dutch deputies were proving more maddening than ever and any attempt he made to develop an offensive strategy collapsed through lack of co-operation. Even Marlborough's patience began to wear thin and he wrote home bitterly to Godolphin, 'I shall not be very fond of staying with an army that is to do no more than eat forage.'

Anne's reaction is not hard to imagine: first Sarah threatening to abandon the Court, and now Marlborough speaking of retirement! Sarah was as necessary to her as was Marlborough to her government and her armies. Every effort had to be made to keep him at his post, and in Winston Churchill's view, the letter she wrote to Sarah in the summer of 1703 'ranks her with Queen Elizabeth and the greatest sovereigns of the English line':

> The thoughts that both my dear Mrs Freeman and Mr Freeman seem to have of retiring give me no small uneasiness, and therefore I must say something on that subject. It is no wonder at all that people in your posts should be weary of the world, who are so continually troubled with all the hurry and impertinences of it; but give me leave to say you should a little consider your faithful friends and poor country, which must be ruined if ever you put your melancholy thoughts in execution. As for your poor, unfortunate, faithful Morley, she could not bear it; for if ever you should forsake me, I would have nothing more to do with the world, but make another abdication; for what is a crown when the support of it is gone? I will never forsake your dear self, Mr Freeman nor Mr Montgomery [Godolphin], but always be your constant and faithful friend, and we four must never part till death mows us down with his impartial hand.

'*We four must never part till death mows us down with his impartial hand*'

But the old circle from the Cockpit needed support in Parliament, where the paradox of a predominantly Tory ministry policy committed to a war on foreign soil was becoming daily more difficult to sustain. When Marlborough returned to England for the winter of 1703–4 the political scene at Whitehall was as irritating as the restrictions of the deputies. A summer's campaigning which had brought no tangible gains inevitably gave strength to Tory dissatisfaction, and when, in the new Parliamentary session, the more extreme among the Tories again introduced their Occasional Conformity Bill, the implications behind it were clear. If the bill passed it would mean the discomfort of the Whigs, while the triumphant Tory extremists would stint supplies for the war, and, at the first opportunity, pull English troops back from the Continent.

In 1702 Anne had favoured the bill, but now she hesitated. The violence of party quarrelling was distressing and her own Tories were as much at fault in this as the Whigs. In her opening speech to Parliament in November Anne had vainly begged that they 'would carefully avoid any Heats and Divisions', but tempers were running high and the session was a stormy one. Even the dogs and cats, according to Swift, were more quarrelsome than usual and 'why should we wonder at that when the very ladies are split asunder into high church and low, and out of zeal for religion have hardly time to say their prayers'. Anne decided to sit on the fence : Prince George, to his relief, was instructed that this time he should not support the bill, and though she declared she 'would have no worse opinion of any of the Lords that are for it', her attitude contributed to its second defeat in the Lords.

The natural sequel was a readjustment of the government, shifting the balance away from the Tory extremists. Nottingham committed political suicide in the mistaken belief that he was indispensable, presenting Anne with an ultimatum : either the Whig Dukes of Somerset and Devonshire should be dismissed, or he would resign. To his amazement, Somerset and Devonshire remained and it was he, Seymour and Jersey (Sarah's Tory high-fliers) who lost their positions instead. Harley became Secretary of State in place of Nottingham, and also secured the appointment of his protégé, a promising young Tory named Henry St John, to the office of Secretary at War, so that St John's considerable talents would be exercised for, and not against, the government. Thus, while Marlborough was fighting his campaign of 1704, he had a firmer backing at home with Godolphin to lead the government, helped by Harley managing the Commons, and a sprinkling of Whigs in the Ministry to lend their voices and their votes to the war effort.

It was backing sorely needed for the plan slowly coming to fruition : Marlborough's mind was daring in the extreme, and not calculated to appeal to the isolationist Tories. The plan itself was a well-kept secret, and even Sarah knew only that he aimed to go 'higher up into Germany'. Anne must have known a little more, for her authorisation was requested to separate the English troops from the Dutch if the latter would not follow Marlborough, but probably even she was not in his full confidence. For by 1704 Marlborough had recognised, with all the genius of a great strategist, that the danger had shifted from the north of Europe to the centre, and that it was not Holland but the Empire which represented the weak link of the Alliance. As the Hungarians revolted in the east and the Elector of Bavaria deserted to the French side in the west, it seemed in the spring of that year as if Vienna itself might fall to Louis's armies. Swift action was needed to prevent such a disastrous blow to the Allied cause, but a lesser man than Marlborough might well have thought the task impossible. Not only were his armies in the Netherlands, over six hundred miles away from the French troops threatening Vienna, but the Dutch desperately wanted to keep all available troops to defend their own land. It required all Marlborough's skill and deception to keep them, as well as the French, from guessing his destination as he struck camp and moved southwards. At first he made a series of feints to the west, appearing as if to attack Lorraine or Alsace, and it was not until he left the line of the Rhine and took a sharp turn to the east that his real intentions were guessed by the French – and not till then were the Dutch and the German princes of the Alliance officially informed of his destination. The march itself was a fantastic feat of organisation : 'Surely,' wrote one English captain, 'there never was such a march carried on with more order and regularity and with less fatigue both to man and horse.' The leading Imperial general, Prince Eugene of Savoy, for whom Marlborough was to develop enormous respect and liking, was also marching his troops towards Bavaria to link up with Marlborough, and it was together that, on 13 August, these two great military leaders fought the French near the Bavarian village of Blenheim.

The tactics of the battle were as original and unorthodox as the daring strategy of the march. Marlborough, in command of the Allied centre and left, while Eugene led the right, ignored the accepted theory that any attack against the enemy centre would be overwhelmed and crushed by the wings, and launched his main offensive from the centre, while still managing to hold the French wings, and by the late afternoon it was clear that the Allies had won. There were reckoned to be about twenty-three thousand enemy casualties, fifteen thousand prisoners, including the French Marshal Tallard, and what was left of their forces retreated in panic through the Black Forest. The myth

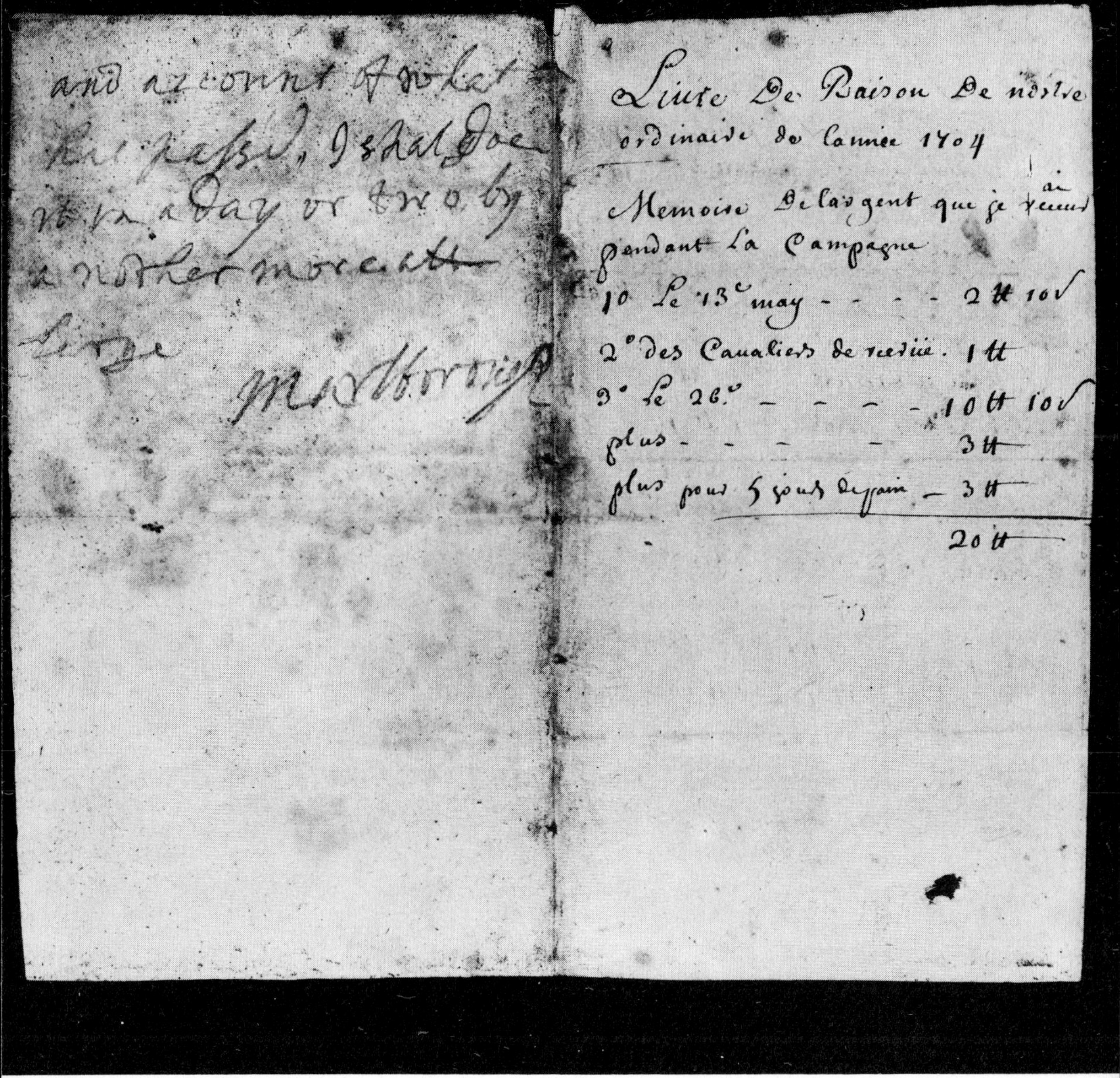

and accompt of what
... pass... I shall do
it ... a day or two by
another morsell

M. Marlbrough

Liure De Raison De nôtre
ordinaire de l'année 1704

Memoire De l'argent que je receu
pendant la Campagne
1° Le 13e may - - - - - 2 lt 10 s
2° des Caualiers de retüe . 1 lt
3° Le 26e - - - - - 10 lt 10 s
plus - - - - 3 lt
plus pour 5 jours de pain — 3 lt
                              20 lt

of French invincibility on the battlefield, accepted in Europe
for two generations, was shattered, and Louis XIV, when he
was finally told, was at first incredulous, and then issued an
edict forbidding all mention of the battle.

Anne received the news at Windsor while, legend has it, she
was playing at dominoes seated in one of the great bay windows
overlooking the Park. It had taken eight days for Marlborough's messenger, Colonel Parke, to ride back across
Europe and then wait for the wind to blow him to England

Political cartoon of 1706, showing Louis XIV
caught between England and Holland, while
William III looks on from above.
On the right, the eagle, representing
William, attacks the cock of France.

120

with his momentous message from the Duke. It was scribbled to his wife on the back of a tavern bill :

> I have not time to say more, but to beg you will give my duty to the Queen, and let her know her army has had a glorious victory. Monsieur Tallard and two other generals are in my coach, and I am following the rest. The bearer, my aide-de-camp, Colonel Parke, will give her an account of what has passed. I shall do it in a day or two by another more at large – Marlborough.

Anne, with tears of joy running down her cheeks, gave Parke a miniature of herself and a thousand guineas in reward. In London copies of Marlborough's note were struck off the presses in their hundreds and the people went mad with joy. 'Mirth sat on every countenance and you might read satisfaction in every face.' It was a land victory such as England had not known since Agincourt, and overnight Marlborough underwent his transformation from a great soldier to a national hero. He was to win other battles, arguably as glorious, and Anne would preside over England's rising fortunes for a decade to come ; but never again would the same unalloyed taste of victory sweep over the nation and bind the people together as it did for a rare moment after the Battle of Blenheim.

5 The Whig War
1704-8

A THANKSGIVING SERVICE for the victory at Blenheim was held at St Paul's Cathedral in September, and Anne and Sarah rode there together. Evelyn, then an old man of eighty-two, described the scene in one of the last entries of his diary: 'The Queen in a rich coach with eight horses, none with her but the Duchess of Marlborough in a very plain garment, the Queen full of jewels. ... The day before was wet and stormy but this was one of the most serene and calm days that had been all the year.'

Anne certainly had good reason to be grateful that the husband of her best friend had turned out to be the greatest general in Europe, and she had already assured Sarah that, next to God Almighty, she considered the victory to be wholly due to 'dear Mr Freeman'. It was tiresome that the Tory 'high-fliers' were exaggerating the role of Prince Eugene and saying that Admiral Rooke's capture of Gibraltar, a few weeks before the battle of Blenheim, was just as important, but the rest of the nation was only too happy to join with Anne in giving full credit to Marlborough.

Inevitably Anne's thoughts turned to a suitable reward. But what? Marlborough was already a duke, so there was no further promotion open to him. Anne envied Emperor Leopold's power to make him a Prince of the Holy Roman Empire, though Sarah did not think much of her new title of Princess of Mindelheim, for she complained she could not even find the place on the map. Clearly something had to be done, and several possibilities were considered, including a statue, a Marlborough Square in London, a London mansion. Finally Anne and Sarah hit on the happy solution of the great country estate he so far lacked, for St Albans, however pleasant, was really far too small for a duke. And so, on 17 February 1705, Anne announced to Parliament that she had decided to grant to the Duke and his heirs the Crown's interest in the Manor of Woodstock, with the sole and picaresque condition that each year the possessor should present to the Queen and her successors, on the anniversary of the battle of Blenheim, a standard emblazoned with three fleurs-de-lis on a field argent, to represent the captured colours of France – an obligation which has been met to this day. Both Houses gratefully voted the necessary supplies to clear the land, and Anne was able to order the build-

y 128 Enſigns & 34 St Blenheime Carried &c dont ſet up in Weſtmr

ABOVE Following the victory at Blenheim, the captured French flags were brought back to England and carried in procession to Westminster Hall.

PREVIOUS PAGES The Battle of Ramillies, Marlborough's victory over Villeroi, which took place in May 1706. As a result of this battle, almost all the Spanish Netherlands fell to the allies.

ABOVE RIGHT
Prince Eugene of Savoy,
the third member
of the 'triumvirate'
with Marlborough
and Heinsius of the
Dutch Republic, against
France. Portrait by
Jacques von Schuppen.

ing at royal expense of a palace which was to be called 'the castle of Blenheim'.

Blenheim Palace is the great monument of the reign. Architecturally, although it involved many of the finest architects and craftsmen of the day, such as Vanbrugh, Hawksmoor, Verrio, Laguerre and Key, it is quite untypical of the traditional styles of the period – the quiet homely elegance of most 'Queen Anne' houses, and the restrained symmetry of Wren and his pupils. To many contemporaries, Blenheim was quite tasteless : 'one mass of stone without taste or relish' was one comment, while to another it appeared a curious hybrid, 'a college with a church in the middle'. Yet the story of Blenheim Palace, in fact, is a unique one, shaped by the characters and relations of

125

Blenheim Palace

Anne decided to build at her own expense a house to be called 'the castle of Blenheim', in reward for Marlborough's great victory. The architect chosen was Sir John Vanbrugh, Wren's second-in-command at the Board of Works, who soon fell out with Sarah. 'I made Mr Vanbrugh my enemy,' declared Sarah, 'by the constant disputes I had with him to prevent his extravagance.' The foundation-stone was laid in 1705, but the building continued for many years. In 1716, Vanbrugh left in a rage; Sarah called upon James Moore and Nicholas Hawksmoor to complete the palace.

ABOVE The medieval royal palace of Woodstock, which had fallen into ruins by the early eighteenth century. The ancient palace had associations with Henry II and his mistress, 'Fair Rosamund'. Vanbrugh wanted to preserve the ruins as of historical interest, but Sarah ordered their demolition.

RIGHT Plan of the gardens at Blenheim at the time of the 1st Duke. The Grand Parterre, lying to the south of the house, was a formal garden, created by Vanbrugh with the help of Henry Wise. It had a military framework of eight bastions and a curtain wall, within which Wise planted evergreens and built arched lime-walks. Marlborough requested that fully-grown trees should be planted in the park, so Wise transplanted 'elms out of the country' into the main avenues to the north and west.

BELOW Aerial view of Blenheim Palace, showing the great forecourt and the Doric north front.

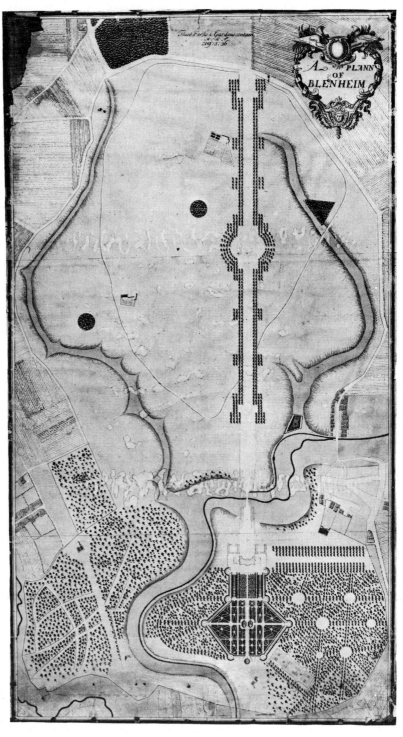

the leading personalities of the reign. To Anne it was at first a magnificent present that she was delighted to give, and then, having inspected the model with George at Kensington, she lost interest and never went near it. Sarah, too, though at first enthusiastic, grew suspicious of the grandiose ostentation and 'the madness of the Whole Design'. This did not stop her from an intense personal involvement. 'I beg of you,' her husband had entreated, 'to do all that you can that the house at Woodstock may be carried up as much as possible, that I may have the prospect of living in it.' And, loyally determined to carry out her husband's wishes whilst he was abroad, she infuriated the workmen by her 'extremely prying-into habits' and, though she launched herself into a fresh crusade against extravagance, at the same time she insisted that everything possible should be done to complete it.

It was, indeed, John's house and not Sarah's. Each winter he would ride over the site to examine the progress, suggest alterations; and each summer would write to Sarah, to Vanbrugh and to Godolphin for news. In the gardens he insisted that fully-grown trees should be planted, for he had not time enough left to him to watch saplings grow, and suggested to Sarah, 'if possible, I should wish that you might or somebody you can rely on taste the fruit of every tree'. Now well into middle age, and very conscious of the fact, he was anxious to make the place his home for his last years. But it was more than that. Beneath Marlborough's bland, unruffled surface, one senses a soaring ambition, and it is at Blenheim that it found expression. It was the nearest England ever approached to rivalling Versailles; it was destined never to be merely a home for a great general to end his days, but a titanic monument to the military prowess of the greatest soldier of the age and from the beginning designed on an imperial scale.

The procedure of building the palace, and paying for it, was amazingly unbusinesslike. It would have seemed ungrateful and ill-bred to inquire precisely how much Anne was prepared to pay for it, and so no one did; never was there anything in the nature of a written agreement between her and Marlborough. Even the choice of architect, Sir John Vanbrugh, looked suspiciously casual and, according to Vanbrugh, he got the job simply because he happened to meet Marlborough at a play-

house in London. Why Sir Christopher Wren, Vanbrugh's
senior at the Queen's Office of Works and in many ways the
obvious candidate, was passed over is not clear. Perhaps Vanbrugh's Whig friends pushed him forward, or perhaps the Duke
had been impressed by the grandiose house he had just built for
the Earl of Carlisle at Castle Howard in Yorkshire. Nonethe-
less, it was Wren who, after Vanbrugh had prepared his model,
was sent off to Woodstock to produce an estimate, and returned
with the staggering news that the Queen's present would cost
her nearly £100,000. Sarah was quite scandalised, but the
Queen declared herself willing to foot this enormous bill, and
Marlborough and Vanbrugh were enthusiastic. So, in June
1705, the foundation stone was laid: 'eight foot square, finely

polished about eighteen inches over, and laid upon it were these words inlayed in pewter: "In memory of the battle of Blenheim, June 18 1705, Anna Regina"'.

Apart from Blenheim, Anne, though no great builder, soon had other projects under way. At Kensington Vanbrugh had designed for her an Orange House, which was completed in 1705, a charming, rather appropriate, memorial to her artistic patronage. With its white interior exquisitely carved by Grinling Gibbons, and surrounded by gardens, it was the perfect setting for supper parties, or for private performances in the small round music room at one end, where guests could listen to the harpsichord, or join in one of d'Urfey's pastoral songs. Anne's gardens, in particular, were proving to be an extravagance. Despite all Sarah's strictures and her own resolutions to cut down expenditure, within the first four years of her reign Anne had laid out over £26,000 on her various gardens and parks. At Kensington the gardens were redesigned by the royal gardener Henry Wise. The box hedges planted by William were uprooted because Anne disliked the smell. More land was taken in, on the upper slopes a kitchen-garden laid out, and, as the *pièce-de-résistance*, old gravel pits were drained and transformed into a sunken garden. The man responsible, Henry Wise, was the leading gardener of the day. Not only was he in charge of the royal parks and gardens, but he was also designing those at Blenheim, and his reputation was such that he 'gave directions once or twice a year in most of the Noblemen's and Gentlemen's gardens in England'.

At Windsor Wise planned and created for Anne a new formal garden on the south side of the Castle, while in the park new walks and avenues were laid out, and care was taken to level the rides through the park where Anne hunted in her chaise. After all, it had been a molehill that had finished off William. At St James's, the canal built for Charles II was widened and Wise, on top of all his other appointments, was also Deputy Ranger. The park was an obvious attraction for Londoners, but there were restrictions on its use. People were not allowed to walk on the grass, to buy or sell anything, or to dry their linen. As for 'ordinary or mean people, beggars or dogs', they were excluded altogether, and even noblemen who abused their special privileges were severely reprimanded.

Coffee-houses reached their zenith of popularity under Anne. Whigs and Tories, merchants and bankers would each have their favourite haunt, but all the houses offered the same attractions: 'you have all manner of news there: you have a good fire, which you may sit by as long as you please; you have a Dish of Coffee; you meet your friends for the transack of Business, and all for a Penny, if you don't care to spend more'.

ABOVE Watercolour of a coffee-house in the late seventeenth century.

LEFT Fighting in a coffee-house in 1710 over the trial of Dr Sacheverell.

It was a pity, Anne felt, that she and Sarah could not discuss such pleasant topics as the lay-out of the new walks at Windsor or Wise's latest schemes for Kensington, but as Sarah advanced into intolerant middle age, her initial ardour for her Court duties had cooled before the boredom of Anne's company. 'It was extremely tedious,' she wrote later, 'to be so much where there could be no manner of conversation.' She preferred the country and her absences increased, but Anne, despite all the other demands on her time, still pursued her incessantly into country, at Holywell, Windsor or Blenheim, with her letters: 'Your faithful Mrs Morley has a mind to come and imagine how they [spa waters] agree with you on Monday if it be convenient or else on Friday sevennight or if you had rather the later end of this week or the beginning of the week after next whatever time is easiest to you and your dear Mr Freeman, do but name it and I shall fly with joy to my dear Mrs Freeman.' When Sarah wrote back to her, not as often as Anne wished, it was often too formally for the Queen's liking: 'I can't help being uneasy that you call me twice Majesty,' she replied on one occasion, 'and not once mention your poor unfortunate faithful Morley.' But Sarah, with twenty years as a royal favourite behind her and now with her husband the victor of Blenheim and her two daughters to represent her at Court, felt less need than ever to keep up the Queen's friendship.

Poor Anne! Her 'sunshine day' had soon clouded over, and with Sarah failing her, and beset as she was with ill health, she was often in low spirits. Her public duties brought little consolation. Marlborough might have raised England's prestige to a new pinnacle abroad, but at home Anne saw little to please her in the political scene. Her hope that the dismissal of the Tory high-fliers in 1704 would lead to a government of moderate men was an impossible dream in an age of party strife.

The battle of Blenheim had momentarily silenced the opposition to the war for it was, as one Tory squire put it, 'more for their four shillings in the pound than they had ever seen before'. But the moment of national rejoicing did not last for long and when Parliament reassembled in the autumn of 1705, for all Anne's pleas for unity and concord, the two parties still found plenty to quarrel about. It was partly in the hope that her presence might induce members to act more moderately that,

in this session, Anne revived Charles II's practice of attending debates in the House of Lords in person, sitting either on the throne or, in the colder months, on a bench beside the fire.

The session of 1704–5 once again saw the introduction of the Tories' Occasional Conformity Bill. This time Nottingham, still smarting from his dismissal, proposed that it should be 'tacked on' to the Land Tax and therefore faced Parliament with the choice of passing it or of foregoing vital supplies for the war. The scheme roused all the fury of party feeling: the Tories were split; Marlborough and Godolphin, though still anxious to uphold the Church, were turning to the Whigs for support of the war, and this time both voted against the bill, while the Queen was openly incensed with the behaviour of the Tory extremists. It was monstrous, she declared, for them to endanger supplies for the war to further their own party ends, and she was delighted when the bill was flung out in the House of Lords.

The natural alternative to the troublesome Tories was some kind of alliance with the Whigs, and both Godolphin and Marlborough were ready to move towards them. Yet the Queen's growing disillusion with Nottingham and his like had not, so far, been accompanied by any softening in her attitude to the Whigs, who were now clamouring louder than ever for office in return for their support of the war. Moderate whigs like the Duke of Newcastle, she was prepared to accept if absolutely necessary, and in March 1705 he replaced Buckingham as Lord

ABOVE The Green House – now called the Orangery – at Kensington Palace, designed for the Queen by Vanbrugh, and completed in 1705. It was used for summer supper parties and musical evenings.

ABOVE RIGHT Kip's view of the formal gardens laid out for William III by London and Wise. The gardens were laid out in the Dutch style, divided up into separate compartments, and without clear focal points.

BELOW RIGHT When Anne came to the throne, she completely changed the gardens, rooting up the box and 'giving an English model to the old-made gardens'. In the background are the new gardens, including the kitchen gardens and sunken garden. This engraving dates from *c.* 1710.

Her Majesties Royal Palace at Kensington

Her most Serene and most Sacred Majesty, ANNE by y^e Grace of God QUEEN of Great Britain, France & Ireland &c.

THE ROYAL PALACE OF KENSINGTON joyns to High Park, and was purchased from the Earl of Nottingham by K. William, who made several additions to it, which caused y^e Building the somewhat irregular without; but its apartments are very fine and well disposed within, containing a curious collection of Original Paintings. The Gardens of this Pallace are very fine and charmingly kept the Front of the Palace on that side is very noble. The Avenue leading from St James's through High Park to this Palace, is very Grand, on each Side of it Lanthorns are placed at equal distances, which being lighted in the Dark Seasons for the conveniency of the Courtiers, appear inconceivably Magnificent.

Henry Wise, the Royal Gardener

In the 1680s, Henry Wise went into partnership with George London, and set up his nursery at Brompton Park. He was greatly influenced by the work of the French royal gardener, Le Nôtre, and quickly became the leading gardener of his day in England. For William III he worked at Kensington and Hampton Court, and for Anne at Kensington, Windsor and St James's. He also designed many of the gardens for the great country houses of the period, including Blenheim.

ABOVE LEFT Godfrey Kneller's portrait of Henry Wise, painted in 1715. LEFT Henry Wise's plan for Marshal Tallard's gardens at Nottingham where, according to legend, celery was grown in England for the first

ABOVE Workmen creating formal gardens in the style of Le Nôtre and Henry Wise.

time. Tallard had been captured at Blenheim, and was kept in captivity at Nottingham, although as a former Ambassador to England, he had many friends there and was treated more like a guest than a prisoner.

137

Privy Seal. But for their leaders she had nothing but fear and dislike, and would not hear of their entering her government.

The Whigs were ruled by a small clique, the so-called 'Lords of the Junto'. There were five of them, and they supplied their party with an organisation and effectiveness that was the envy of the divided Tories. These men were hardly the irresponsible devils of Anne's imagination. Lord Somers was one of the most distinguished lawyers ever to sit on the Woolsack, Lord Halifax had, under William, enjoyed a spectacular career at the Exchequer and Treasury, and Lord Orford, as Admiral Russell, was the victor of Cape La Hogue in 1692. But it was the other two members of the group whom Anne most detested, and who distorted her judgment of the other three, and of the whole Whig party. Lord Tom Wharton, 'bluff, blasphemous and randy', was one of the most colourful personalities of the age, an extraordinary mixture 'of the very best and of the very worst'. As a politician his mastery of electioneering was equalled by none, and he was one of the very few members of either House who would never bend his political principles to gain favour or office. Yet in his private life Wharton was flagrantly

Three members of the Whig clique, the 'Lords of the Junto'. Left to right: John Somers, Lord Chancellor: portrait by Godfrey Kneller, c. 1700–10.
Charles Montagu, 1st Earl of Halifax, Chancellor of the Exchequer and First Lord of the Treasury: portrait by Godfrey Kneller for the Kit-Cat Club, c. 1703–10.
Thomas Wharton, 1st Marquess of Wharton, portrait by Godfrey Kneller, c. 1710 for the Kit-Cat Club.

immoral, a foul-mouthed atheist who had once, it was rumoured, defecated in a church pulpit, and was one of the greatest rakes of the day. It was his scandalous reputation that, in Anne's upright, if slightly priggish view, totally disqualified him for any public office and confirmed her worst suspicions about the wickedness of the Whigs.

The fifth member of the Junto was the young Lord Sunderland who, as Sarah's son-in-law, might have been expected to enjoy a useful passport to royal favour. But Anne detested him almost as much as she loathed Wharton. Of the five, Sunderland was the most extreme in his views and made no secret either of his suspicion of royal prerogatives, or of his contempt for Anne personally. He scorned to make any overtures to her and had aroused her undying resentment by his leading part in the opposition to a bill granting Prince George an income for life. In vain did Sarah plead that he might be admitted to a government office and reprove Anne for her unbending attitude to the Whigs. 'I have the same opinion of Whig and Tory that I ever had,' wrote Anne firmly in November 1705. 'I know their principles very well and when I know myself to be in the right nothing can make me alter mine.' No one could accuse her of misreading her own character.

But for the summer at least Anne could forget about the Lords of the Junto. Under the terms of the Triennial Act, her first Parliament was nearing the end of its life and in March she finally dissolved it, reproaching it for the 'unreasonable humour and animosity, the fatal effects of which we have so narrowly escaped in this session', and expressing the unlikely hope that its successor would be less quarrelsome. With the country now busily preparing for a general election and no Parliament to bother about until the autumn, Anne could briefly enjoy some of the pleasures of being Queen and, a few days after the dissolution, accompanied by George, she set out for Newmarket. Horse-racing had been firmly established as a royal pastime by Charles II, and Anne, from her girlhood, had often attended meetings, though it was a sport that was becoming associated with the Whigs rather than with the Tories, who generally stuck to fox-hunting, and complained that it was only the rich Whigs who could afford good enough horses for racing. The price of a race-horse was certainly high, even in those days, and when, on this visit, Anne bought one called *Leeds* for George, it cost her a thousand guineas. But she was, after all, the richest woman in England and could afford to pay for her pleasures – particularly if Sarah was not watching.

The general election held that summer prompted a fierce, and often violent, conflict between the parties. At Coventry the High Tory candidates tried to dictate the result by seizing the town hall for the three days of polling, and knocking on the head any Whigs who tried to get in to vote, while at Chester a Whig mob smashed in the cathedral windows as a gesture against 'the Church Party'. Anne's hopes for harmony in the new Parliament were remote and, to her dismay, she found that her name, too, had been dragged into the field of electioneering, when a High Tory tract appeared, entitled *A Memorial to the Church of England*, attacking her, Godolphin and Marlborough as enemies of the Church. The pamphlet was publicly burned by the hangman, but it was a nasty blow to a Queen who prided herself on her identity with the Church. The tract was just one more indication that the honeymoon period between the Crown and the Tories was over, and the government's move away from the 'high-fliers' had helped to tip the electoral balance ; so that the result of this election was a mild triumph for the Whigs.

When the new Parliament assembled in the autumn, Godolphin and Harley found that it was much easier to get bills of supply for the war safely through the Commons ; but for Anne it also meant that the pressure to give the Whigs government offices increased, and over this Godolphin and Harley were not wholly in agreement. Harley, like Anne, disliked extremes and felt that further moves towards the Whigs would place the Crown dangerously in their power. 'The foundation is persons and parties are to come to the Queen and not the Queen to them,' he wrote to Godolphin. 'If the gentlemen of England are made sensible that the Queen is the head and not a party, everything will be easy, and the Queen will be courted and not a party.' But Godolphin thought differently : 'Is it not more reasonable and more easy to preserve those who have served and helped us than those who have basely and ungratefully done all that was in their power to ruin us ?' During the early years of the reign it was almost impossible to distinguish between

ABOVE RIGHT Sarah had always occupied apartments near the Queen in St James's Palace, but in 1709, she decided that she would like a town-house of her own. She persuaded the Queen to grant her a lease of land on the eastern edge of the palace, and asked Wren to design Marlborough house. She avoided Vanbrugh because they were already quarrelling over Blenheim Palace, but quickly fell out with Wren too, and eventually finished the house herself.

The exterior has been
greatly altered, but the
Saloon retains much of
its eighteenth-century
splendour. Above the
cornice are Laguerre's
paintings of the
Battle of Blenheim.

RIGHT Marlborough
studying a plan of the
siege of Bouchain with his
chief engineer, Colonel
Armstrong. Sarah later
declared that this portrait,
by Seeman, was 'as like
him as ever I saw'.

Anne's hand and that of Godolphin in the matter of appointments and dismissals, but now Godolphin's conciliatory attitude to the Whigs, coupled with Anne's continuing hostility, created a rift which, though it did not yet affect Godolphin's own position, threw Anne's personal views into sharper relief.

The first battle was over the appointment of Lord Cowper, a moderate Whig and a man of impeccable integrity, whom Anne eventually admitted to finding very agreeable. But in 1705, when he was put forward for the sensitive position of Lord Keeper, who advised the Crown on Church appointments, she wrote pleadingly to Godolphin : 'I cannot help saying I wish very much that there may be a moderate Tory found for this employment.'

Pressure from Godolphin, backed by Marlborough, eventually forced Anne to accept the Whig, but the episode was an indication of the cracks that were appearing in the early harmony of the reign. But to Anne the most distressing political event of the autumn was the debate on the question of the succession. She was now forty and had not conceived for over five years, and it was clear that only a miracle could give her another child. The Act of Settlement had already laid down that the Crown should pass to the Hanoverians, but in November a Tory peer, Lord Haversham, put forward a motion proposing that the Electress Sophia and her grandson George should be invited to come to England immediately. Such a step, it was argued, would damage the hopes of any Jacobite rising and would also introduce the Electress and her family to England. It would seem at first sight to be a perfectly sensible suggestion and Sophia, though over seventy, announced herself willing to co-operate. Yet, as ever, party squabbles were at the back of the plan, for Haversham and his Tory supporters were well aware that Anne strongly disliked her Hanoverian relations and were trying to put Marlborough, Godolphin and the Whigs in an awkward position. On the one hand, if they supported the motion, they would offend Anne, but on the other, if they opposed it, they would apparently be neglecting their declared support for the Protestant succession and would certainly be offending their future monarch. The Tories congratulated themselves on the manœuvre and welcomed a debate, certain to embarrass their opponents.

142

It took some courage for Anne to attend. The subject was one which involved her deepest emotions, for it touched on all the most sensitive areas of her life ; on all her dead children, especially Gloucester ; on her attitude to her father, and to his son, the Old Pretender ; on her resentment of George of Hanover's rejection of her over twenty years before; and, of course, on her own death. And Parliament spared her nothing. When Haversham asked, 'Is there any man, My Lords, who doubts that if the Duke of Gloucester had been alive, Her Majesty had not been more secure than she is?', Anne was so overcome at the mention of her 'poor boy's' name that she had to withdraw. While the debate lasted she was said to have wept for three days and three nights, yet she was present to hear Buckingham suggest that it would be well to make such arrangements to deal with the possibility that she might become senile in old age.

But the Whigs, by a clever manœuvre, instigated by one of the Junto, Somers, managed to defeat the proposal by substituting a Regency Act, by which it was agreed that, on Anne's death, the government of the country would be placed in the hands of the Lords Justices until the new sovereign arrived from Hanover. The Tories found they had done little more than weaken their position still further for, as Anne wrote to Sarah : 'I believe Dear Mrs Freeman and I shall not disagree as we have formerly done, for I am sensible of the services those people have done me that you have a good opinion of and will countenance them, and am marvellously convinced of the malice and insolence of them that you have always been speaking against.' Anne was not by any means ready to fall into the arms of the Junto, but it marked an important change in her attitude.

The continuation of the war, too, helped to strengthen the Whig position. As England became increasingly committed, so those men who gave it their support became ever more necessary. For Marlborough the year after Blenheim was one of setbacks and frustration. In the spring of 1705 he wanted to attack the French across the Rhine and, if possible, carry the war into France itself, but the Dutch deputies, 'these sad fellows, great pedants', refused to support his plan. The Emperor, too, failed to provide the help he had promised and on all sides Marlborough felt his command hemmed in and undermined by the behaviour of his allies.

143

It was in Spain that England fought the most decisive action that year. To start with, things went badly there too, then in the late summer the Earl of Peterborough, with an English and Dutch fleet and with the Allied candidate for the Spanish throne, Charles III, sailed up the east coast of Spain and, after far more quarrels with his allies than Marlborough ever had, managed to capture Barcelona and thereby trigger off a chain of revolts against Philip in Catalonia. For the first time it seemed to the Allies as if there was a definite prospect of ousting Philip and yet, in retrospect, it was an unfortunate victory, for by committing the Allies to winning in Spain for Charles, it thereby ensured the prolongation of the war. It was not an aim that had been one of the original articles of the Grand Alliance in 1701, which had wanted to partition the Empire between Charles and Philip, and, as it proved, they never managed to achieve it. But 'No peace without Spain!' became part of the Whig creed and a major obstacle in all attempts to negotiate a peace. Even when, in 1707, Marlborough's nephew, the Duke of Berwick at the head of the French armies in Spain inflicted a crushing defeat on the Allies at Almanza and virtually ended all prospect of Charles becoming King, the Whigs refused to abandon it.

For the moment, though, the Whigs' fortunes at home were rising, for there was yet another matter, besides the war, in which the Tory Queen found herself looking to them for support. The project of uniting the Parliaments of England and Scotland had been under discussion since the Revolution of 1688, and it was a design to which Anne, guided by Godolphin, gave her blessing; and one which was opposed by many anti-Presbyterian Tories. During 1703 the Scots passed an Act of Security, laying down that when Anne died the Scots Parliament should meet to choose her successor, who was to be a Protestant of the royal line, but not necessarily the head of the House of Hanover. The dangers for England were obvious. It was not impossible that the Pretender would renounce his Catholicism and, if he became King in Scotland while England and France were still at war, Louis XIV might easily exploit Scotland as a back-door into England. And even if the Pretender did remain a Catholic, the Scottish Highlands were known to be full of Jacobites who would ignore the clause about Pro-

OPPOSITE Michael Dahl's portrait of Anne, painted in about 1690, when she was in her mid-twenties.

145

testantism and rush a Catholic James III to Edinburgh to be crowned.

It was undoubtedly in the interests of English security for the kingdoms to be united. The English Parliament, therefore, on the initiative of the Whig Junto, replied to the Scots' Act by passing an Aliens Act, authorising Anne to appoint commissioners to negotiate a union, but also stipulating that from Christmas Day 1705, until the Scottish Parliament settled the Crown upon the admitted successor in England, Scotsmen should be treated as aliens in England and that trade across the border should be drastically restricted. As Scotland depended heavily on its commercial links with England, this was an effective riposte and, in April 1706, thirty-one commissioners from each kingdom assembled in London to begin the new negotiations. Anne attended several of the sessions of the commissioners and one of them, Sir John Clerk has left a vivid and pathetic description of her:

> Her Majesty was labouring under a fit of the Gout, and in extreme pain and agony, and on this occasion everything about her was much in the same disorder as about the meanest of her subjects. Her face which was red and spotty, was rendered something frightful by her negligent dress, and the foot affected was tied up with a pultis and some nasty bandages. I was much affected by this sight ...

While the commissioners argued, England thrilled to another great Marlborough victory. At Ramillies in Flanders, in May 1706, the Duke contrived to defeat the French army under Villeroi, one of the less able of the French generals. The Allies lost only some four thousand men against fifteen thousand Frenchmen killed. Thousands of prisoners were taken, the French guns and their baggage train too, and their army was utterly shattered. The overall effect of the victory was that virtually all the Spanish Netherlands fell into the hands of the Allies, and Marlborough gained in the space of an afternoon what all the years of William's plodding campaigning had failed to win. In England the news was rapturously received: 'most people move about as in a dream or ecstasy, God does so many marvels for us!' Sarah was one of the first to hear of it, and the day after the battle Marlborough wrote to her:

'Alarm at Versailles', a political cartoon of 1706, showing the consternation at the French Court over Marlborough's victory at Ramillies. Louis has fallen to the ground, while at the back to the left stand James, Duke of Berwick, James II's illegitimate son by Arabella Churchill, and his half-brother, James Francis Stuart, the Old Pretender.

147

I did not tell my dearest soul in my last, the design I had of engaging the enemy if possible to a battle, fearing the concern she had for me might make her uneasy, but I can now give her the satisfaction of letting her know that, on Sunday last we fought, and that God Almighty has been pleased to give us a victory. ... Pray believe me when I assure you that I love you more than I can express.

'God Almighty has been pleased to give us a victory'

It was a re-enactment of the national mood after Blenheim, with another thanksgiving at St Paul's and, yet again, of further rewards. There could be no second gift on the same grandiose scale, but Marlborough was granted the £5,000 a year in perpetuity previously withheld by Parliament, and special provision was made for the dukedom to descend through the female line, as the Duke and his Duchess had sadly realised that no son would ever succeed to their inheritance.

From Europe there came the prospect of a more glittering award: the post of Viceroy of the Spanish Netherlands, offered by the Emperor, which Marlborough dearly wished to accept. As usual, he found an objective reason to support his own ambition – he could use the prestige conferred on him to bind the Empire more closely to England. But both he and the Emperor had overlooked the feelings of the Dutch. Control of the Spanish Netherlands touched a sensitive nerve and not even Marlborough was thought fit for the task. There was a stormy scene in the States General, and Heinsius told him that they were not prepared to relinquish this strategically important neighbouring territory to anybody. So, disappointed, but with perfect dignity, Marlborough declined the offer, though as a result, his relations with the Dutch suffered a significant setback.

While her husband had been earning his triumphs abroad, Sarah had, no less determinedly, though with far less tact, continued her battles at home on behalf of the Whigs. The co-operation of the Junto over both the union with Scotland and supplies for the war had given them every hope of entering in strength into government positions. Sunderland, they demanded, should be made Secretary of State in place of the Tory Sir Charles Hedges, and Godolphin was prepared to accept the change. But not Anne. Sunderland might be Sarah's son-in-law, but her dislike of him personally was coupled with her conviction that any further move towards the Whigs would be 'throwing myself into the hands of a party'. She resisted all pressure, though right through the summer and autumn Sarah campaigned on his behalf. Her tactics were sadly inferior to her husband's. Anne might have responded to an appeal based on friendship, affection, personal interest as a mother-in-law, but Sarah firmly based her appeal on reason. She was at pains to deny that her advocacy of Sunderland had anything to do with his being her son-in-law, and declared her views to be based purely on what she believed to be best for the country :

> Your security and the nation's is my chief wish and I beg of God Almighty as sincerely as I shall do for his pardon at my last hour that Mr and Mrs Morley may see their errors as to this notion before it is too late ; but considering how little impression anything makes that comes from your faithful Freeman, I have troubled you too much and I beg your pardon for it.

By any standards, this was a snide and injudicious letter, and the effects were made worse by Sarah's sprawling handwriting which led Anne to misread 'their errors as to this *notion*' as 'their errors to this *nation*' and, therefore, to think that Sarah was dealing her a much bigger insult. She was hurt and angry. After a long silence on Anne's side, and then another tactless letter from Sarah, Godolphin was called in to explain the misunderstanding and patch the matter up. But, as one historian has dryly put it, 'a friendship which is endangered by this misreading of a vowel may safely be said to have passed its prime'.

By the close of the year Anne's stout resistance to the Whigs was weakening, and in December she at last gave way over Sunderland. He replaced Hedges and, though Anne at first clung to the hope that the appointment would silence the Whigs, as she had always feared at heart it did nothing of the kind, and his appointment was followed by that of all the other members of the Junto, except the ageing Halifax. For the next few years it was the Whigs who directed English policy.

The Whigs' triumph meant danger for Harley, whose opposition to them was suspected, if not definitely known. As early as August the Junto had warned one another that he was their leading enemy, and his position was weakened by the rift with Godolphin which, as we have seen, went back to the latter's partial reconciliation with the Whigs. By the summer of 1707 the correspondence between the two men shows Harley

149

The Early Days of Horse Racing

Charles II was passionately fond of horse racing, and converted Newmarket into a thriving racing town, with all the prestige of royal patronage. Anne inherited her uncle's interest in the sport, and frequently visited Newmarket, first as a Princess, and then as Queen. She kept several horses herself, running them under her own name, or that of her trainer, Tregonwell Frampton. In August 1711, she held the first race meeting at Ascot.

ABOVE RIGHT
The Godolphin Arabian, one of the three famous stallions from whom all modern English thoroughbreds are descended in the male line. He was owned by Francis, 2nd Earl of Godolphin, whose father shared Anne's interest in racing. The Godolphin Arabian was kept at Godolphin's Cambridgeshire seat, Gogmagog.
RIGHT The last race run before Charles II at Datchet Mead, with Windsor Castle in the background. The King watches the race from the royal box, in front of which stand the jockeys' scales. The racecourse at Datchet was much patronised by Charles, but was probably abandoned when Anne inaugurated the course at Ascot.

150

ABOVE Tregonwell
Frampton, who served as
trainer-manager to
Charles II, William III,
Anne, and the first two
Georges. He did much to
make Newmarket the
principal centre of racing
in England. Painting by
John Wootton.

anxiously trying to assure Godolphin of his loyalty: 'I have no attachment to any other person in the world but your Lordship and the Duke of Marlborough.' He had a formidable enemy in Sarah, who, with her fervour for throwing blame whole-heartedly on whoever she disliked most at the time, held him to be wholly responsible for Anne's opposition to Sunderland.

Sarah felt nothing but hostility towards Harley, yet ironically, it was she who provided him with a private access to the Queen's counsels. Sarah had a poor relation, Abigail Hill, to whom she had in the past behaved very charitably, if a little condescend-ingly. For some time Abigail had lived with her at St Albans, where Sarah had nursed her through smallpox. When Anne was still a Princess, Sarah had secured a place for Abigail as a woman of the Bedchamber, a position far lower in the Court hierarchy than Lady of the Bedchamber, but none the less, for the daughter of a bankrupt, a valuable position. Abigail seems to have been a sly, undistinguished woman. In Winston Churchill's opinion, she was 'probably the smallest person who ever consciously attempted to decide, and in fact decided, the history of Europe'. A contemporary, the Earl of Dartmouth, found her 'exceedingly mean and vulgar in her manners, childishly exceptious …'. Yet, at least she had ability enough to recommend herself to Anne. Possibly her success lay in the ways in which she differed from Sarah. Where Sarah was arrogant and offhand, Abigail was insinuating and eager to please; Sarah, by this time, made no effort to amuse or comfort the Queen, but Abigail had two useful talents in that she could play delightfully on the harpsichord, and was an excellent mimic; and while Sarah pestered Anne about the Whigs, Abigail was a Tory. Abigail was so unobtrusive that it is hard to date her rise, but in the years after Blenheim, as Sarah's absences from Court increased, so Anne turned more and more to Abigail.

Sarah was far too arrogant to detect a rival for the Queen's favour in this quiet woman. On the contrary, she saw Abigail as a useful asset and one who would look after her interests and deputise for her while she was away. According to one con-temporary account, 'the Duchess grew weary on several accounts of a close attendance she thought she might securely ease herself [of] by leaving near her royal mistress a dependent relation in whom she entirely confided'.

Early in 1707 Abigail married an equerry of Prince George, Samuel Masham, and though Anne attended the ceremony, which was held in Dr Arbuthnot's rooms, it was kept a secret for several months, and Sarah did not hear of it until the summer. A little surprised at not having been told before, she was, nevertheless, prepared to attribute the concealment to Abigail's 'bashfulness and want of breeding' and wished her well. But then she offered to break the news to Anne, and when Abigail informed her that Anne already knew, Sarah began to grow suspicious. Suddenly, at Anne's own clumsy remark, 'I have a hundred times bid Mrs Masham to tell it you and she would not', Sarah grasped the situation. Abigail had become 'an absolute favourite' with constant access to the Queen and no one, least of all Abigail or Anne, had warned her. When she taxed Abigail with supplanting her, insult followed injury; for Abigail patronisingly replied 'that she was sure the Queen who had always loved me extremely would always be very kind to me'. Sarah was outraged: 'To see a woman whom I had raised out of the Dust put on such a Superior air. ...' It was almost too much to bear, but there was nothing she could do about it. Anne, it is true, attempted a reconciliation: 'for I am on the rack and cannot bear living as we do now, being with the same sincere tender passion that I ever was my dear dear Mrs Freeman and shall be so inviolably to my last moment'. But Sarah remained morose and unforthcoming to the point at which their exchanges dissolved into a welter of accusations and renewed recriminations.

'To see a woman whom I had raised out of the Dust put on such a Superior air'

The year had not been a good one for Anne. Abroad, Marlborough was confronted by Marshal Vendôme, an abler man than Villeroi, who did not repeat the mistake of allowing Marlborough to draw him into battle, but held him back before the fortresses of the French frontier. And from Spain there had come news of the disastrous Allied defeat at the battle of Almanza in April. Yet the end of the year did bring one happy event. The Union with Scotland was finally accepted by both Parliaments and by the Scots; and in November Anne drove to Whitehall to open the first Parliament of Great Britain. It was, she said later, 'the happiness of her reign', and was certainly its most enduring domestic achievement. In the looming struggles ahead it was as well that the island was a united one.

Upon her Knees fam'd *Somerset* receives,
An Office which another D——ſs leaves.

6
A Friendship
Ends
1708-11

THE UNION WITH SCOTLAND, gratifying as it was to Anne personally, was naturally detested by Jacobite Scots; and Louis XIV glimpsed the exciting prospect of opening a new front within his enemy's borders. At hand was the ideal instrument, young James, whose birth had precipitated his father's crisis twenty years before. And so, in the early months of 1708, a French fleet, anxiously observed by English spies, assembled at Dunkirk, and at the beginning of March the House of Commons was formally told of the projected invasion and of the arrival at Dunkirk of the 'Pretended Prince of Wales'. As Anne, laid up with gout, waited at Kensington, measures were taken to meet the threat. A proclamation declared 'the Pretended Prince, and all his accomplices, adherents, abettors and advisers to be traitors and Rebels . . .'. All Catholics were under suspicion and the recusancy laws against them were revived, obliging them to remain within five miles of their homes. The Abjuration Oath was re-administered, Habeas Corpus was suspended, and in the northern counties, where the danger would be most acute, the lords-lieutenant were instructed to secure 'all Papists, non-jurors and disaffected persons' and to seize all arms and horses they suspected of going north to Scotland. Anne, for the only time in her reign – and also for the last time in British history – was called upon to exercise the royal prerogative of veto and stopped a Scottish militia bill from becoming law in case the troops so raised were used against her. It was, as it proved, a constitutional landmark, but at the time it was so much part of the general preparations that it aroused no opposition or controversy.

The Prince who was challenging his half-sister's throne was now twenty years old. Tall and dark, he was said to resemble his uncle Charles II in appearance, though his character was considered rather cold and reserved, and there were complaints that he was 'too much under his mother's thumb' and that she had tried to turn him into a saint instead of a king. Anne, of course, had not seen young James since he was a baby; and the fiction that he was not a member of the royal family was busily revived and publicised. Yet now, when he was trying with French troops to wrest at least one of her kingdoms from her, Anne gave a sign that she was painfully conscious of the relationship between them. When, at a meeting of her Council, the

PREVIOUS PAGES The end of the friendship between the Queen and Sarah Churchill, as depicted on a playing card of the period. The Queen gives to the Duchess of Somerset Sarah's Court appointments.

OPPOSITE Anne's half-brother, James Francis Stuart, painted by the studio of A. S. Belle in about 1712.

157

question was raised whether James should be executed if he were captured, Anne became so moved she could not bear to discuss the subject and the meeting had to break up with the question still unsettled.

But, after all the preparations, the invasion proved an anti-climax. The unfortunate Pretender, while his fleet was assembling, had been incubating measles, and the rash erupted just as the fleet was about to set sail. It took him an effort to write a brief line to his mother, 'the body is very feeble but the spirit is so strong it will bear up. I hope not to write to you again until I do so from Edinburgh castle'. Yet James never managed to set foot in Scotland. The French fleet evaded the English under Sir George Byng, but when they arrived in the Firth of Forth the expected signals from the shore never appeared, and so much time was wasted that Byng caught up with them, chasing them north, and, after an argument with his advisers, the Pretender agreed to return to France.

The invasion scare had done more than simply alarm the Queen and confront her with the agonising thought of renewed conflict within her own family. It had played into the hands of the Whigs, who used every opportunity to strengthen their position as the party of loyalty to Anne and of the war. Even before the Pretender made his sad voyage back to France they had engineered a great victory : the fall of Harley, and with him their last powerful enemy in the confidence of the Queen. Harley's dismissal was a personal blow to Anne, and one she resented bitterly. But as she had been unable to prevent Sunderland's appointment, so now she was unable to save Harley. The Whigs had quickly isolated him as their main enemy in the ministry and had been openly gunning for him for some time while he drifted apart from Marlborough and Godolphin. Then, at the end of 1707, with Harley's political foundations increasingly shaky, an espionage scandal was uncovered in his office as Secretary of State, which, though unimportant in itself, provided further fatal ammunition for his Whig opponents. The investigating Lords Committee, consisting entirely of Whigs, was more than ready to seize any shred of evidence against Harley, but found that a poorly-paid clerk named Greg had been responsible and his crime had been a solitary affair. It was impossible to find Harley guilty of anything more heinous

158

than administrative negligence. Even so, the scandal was an ill-timed blow and it enabled his enemies to strike. In February Anne was confronted by a straight choice between keeping Harley, or Godolphin and Marlborough. If he stayed, then they would resign. She put up a stout fight. At one stage she told St John that she had decided to dismiss Godolphin instead, but when Marlborough took up his stand beside the Treasurer, she was beaten. Before a meeting of her Council in February, first Godolphin, then Sarah and then Marlborough, 'lamenting that he came in competition with so vile a creature', came to give their resignations if Harley stayed. Anne tried to stall, ordering Godolphin and Sarah to think over their decisions until the next day, but to Marlborough she said that if he insisted on resigning his Sword of Office 'you will run it through my heart'. It was true, for he was irreplaceable. When neither he nor Godolphin followed her into the Cabinet Room, and the Council opened without them, and with Harley reading a report, 'the Duke of Somerset rose and said if Her Majesty suffered that fellow [pointing to Harley] to treat affairs of the war without the advice of the General, he could not serve her; and so left the Council'. Other Whig ministers followed him and Anne withdrew from the room in distress. Even so, she still clung on a little longer. Harley himself realised that Marlborough and Godolphin had proved a match for him and said he should go, but even so it was not until the Commons had rejected a bill of supply that Anne was finally persuaded to dismiss him, and then 'not without tears in private', as Sarah waspishly commented.

Following their triumphs, the Whigs confidently and correctly predicted that the May elections would see them return in still greater strength. The Tories were more than ever vulnerable to taunts about their Jacobitism, and after Harley's fall the Junto lost no time in pressing further appointments. As Anne had feared, Sunderland's appointment had only paved the way for further demands, and now it was Somers who they were pushing for the post of Lord President of the Council. And although Anne declared to Marlborough that such an appointment would be 'utter destruction to me', she was once again forced to give way, and within the next two years not only Somers but all the other members of the Junto except Halifax had entered her ministry.

'Can she think ...
that the tatling
voice will not in
a little time
make us the jest
of the town?'

There was little comfort to be had in her private life. By now Sarah provided no support at all, for approaching fifty, and with all hope of a son gone for good, she was becoming more and more of a termagant. Her hot temper had become notorious and a regular target for the Tory Press. The unfortunate Bishop Burnet, on being requested by her to explain a lampoon comparing Marlborough to the Roman Count Belisarius, blurted out that Belisarius, too, 'had a brimstone of a wife'. She went on quarrelling with Anne and attacking Abigail, and yet at the same time demanding that all her Court appointments should be inherited by her daughters. Before Marlborough left for Flanders, Anne wrote to him begging him to persuade Sarah to behave in a more friendly way towards her. It was not, after all, an unreasonable letter:

> Can she think ... that the tatling voice will not in a little time make us the jest of the town? Some people will blame her, others me, and a great many both. What a disagreeable noise she will be the occasion of making in the world besides, God knows of what ill consequences it may be. Therefore, for God Almighty's sake, endeavour all you can to persuade Mrs Freeman out of this strange unreasonable resolution.

But Marlborough, too, was finding Sarah difficult. In April he spoke of her 'resolution of living with that coldness and indifferency for me which if it continues must make me the unhappiest man alive'. And although he knew that the quarrel between Anne and Sarah would be interpreted among the Allies as a sign of his own declining favour, he could do nothing about it. After he had left for the Continent, Sarah wrote to tell Anne she had retired into the country, 'since by your very hard and uncommon usage of me, you have convinced all sorts of people, as well as myself, that nothing would be so uneasy to you as my near attendance'.

Anne, as usual, spent the summer at Windsor, according to Sarah because it was easier there for Abigail to smuggle in unseen visitors. Abigail still provided Harley with an approach to the Queen, all the more valuable now that he had been dismissed, and the two corresponded busily all summer, using a transparent code – 'Aunt Stephens' for Anne, and for Sarah, 'My Lady Pye'.

> Oh my poor Aunt Stephens [Abigail told Harley] is to be pitied

very much, for they press her harder than ever. Since what happened lately she is altered more than is to be imagined, no ready
money [firmness] at all to supply her with common necessaries;
really I see it so bad, and they come so fast upon her, I have no hopes
of her deliverance, for she will put it quite out of her friends' power
to save her.

It was at Windsor that Anne heard the news that once more
Marlborough had won a great victory against the French at
Oudenarde. Admittedly for once he owed much to the mistakes of the enemy, but the victory enabled him for the first
time to lead his army into France, into Artois and Picardy, and
to capture Lille, the biggest of the French frontier fortresses,
which finally fell on 9 December. Anne's letter of congratulations to him read as graciously as her thanks to him after
Blenheim: 'I want words to express the joy I have that you are
well after your glorious success for which, next to God Almighty, my thanks are due to you; and indeed I can never say
enough for all the great and faithful services you have ever
done me.'

Yet, ironically, the victory provided the occasion for a
renewed bout of quarrelling between Anne and Sarah, and
also – ominously – for a rift between Anne and Marlborough
himself. Predictably enough, it was a rash action of Sarah's that
provoked the ill-feeling. She had developed a dangerous habit
of showing other people's letters to her, and she now forwarded
to Anne a letter Marlborough had written her in haste after the
battle: 'I do thank God for his goodness in protecting and
making me the instrument of so much happiness to the Queen
and the nation if she will please to make use of it.' Although he
had certainly never intended that Sarah should pass it on, it
sounded harmless enough, but Anne touchily took exception
to the last phrase – 'if she will please to make use of it'. What did
this mean? Would he please explain? When Marlborough
followed up this misunderstanding with some direct advice to
her to 'forgive and to have no more resentments to any particular person or party', she interpreted it as an insulting attempt
to push her further towards the Whigs and reiterated her
determination not to 'put myself entirely into the hands of
one party'.

But with Sarah there was worse to come. The thanksgiving

Political cartoon in the form of a backgammon game between Brabant and Flanders. This refers to the campaigns of 1708, which included the Battle of Oudenarde and the taking of Lille.

for Oudenarde was held in August, and Anne felt it was her duty to make the journey from Windsor to London to be present. But if she had hoped it would be a joyful occasion she was to be disappointed, for Sarah provoked the most painful and public row that they had yet had. As Mistress of the Robes, it was her task to lay out the jewels for Anne to wear but, for some reason, Anne never put them on. The procession started out for St Paul's with both women in the same coach, and then, just before they reached the Cathedral, Sarah noticed that Anne was not wearing the jewels. She did not wait until they were in

162

The Magistrates of Oudenard wait upon the D. of Marlboro desire his protection & swear fidelity to K.C.y iii June the 3. 1706.

private, but attacked Anne on the steps of the Cathedral and then, when Anne tried to explain, rudely told her to be quiet.

It was unforgiveable, and yet it was Sarah, not Anne, who felt justified in writing to complain, laying the blame on Abigail, who was in fact not even in London, but in the country awaiting the birth of a child: '... when I had taken so much pains to put your jewels in a way that I thought you would like, Mrs Masham could make you refuse to wear them, in so un-kind a manner ...'. She also sent on another letter which had come to her from Marlborough. In comparison, Anne's snub-

In June 1708, Marlborough won his third great victory against the French at Oudenarde. This playing card shows the magistrates of Oudenarde waiting upon the Duke.

163

bing reply seems restrained: 'After the commands you gave me on the thanksgiving day of not answering you, I should not have troubled you with these lines, but to return the Duke of Marlborough's letter safe into your hands, and for the same reason do not say anything to that, nor to yours which enclosed it.'

The breach boded ill for the Whigs. On the surface the Junto appeared to be getting their way, but they stood on brittle foundations and knew it. They had forced themselves into power by making themselves necessary to Marlborough and Godolphin, but now it seemed as if Marlborough and Godolphin, too, might well not be necessary to the Queen for all that much longer, and rumours were rife about Anne's secret contacts with Harley. Marlborough's spectacular victories were no longer enough to silence the protests at home. As the war dragged on, demands for peace were growing. Tentative negotiations had been going on for some time and early in 1709, with France weakened by one of the severest winters in living memory, it seemed as if they had every hope of success. That they foundered was not the fault of Louis, but of the Allies, and in particular the English Whigs. Louis gave his consent to all the 'Preliminary Articles' which the Allies drew up to list all their demands, except one. For as far as Spain was concerned, the Allies demanded that not only should Louis cede Spain to Charles, to which he (though not his grandson Philip) was prepared to agree, but that if Philip was still in Spain three months after the signature of the treaty, then the Allies would renew the war – and they would do so strengthened by all the other concessions they claimed from Louis in the projected treaty. Ultimately it would mean that Louis would go to war against Philip, and was a quite unreasonable demand. 'If I continue the war,' he said, 'it is better to contend with my enemies than with my own family.'

So, once again, as spring arrived the armies of Europe took up their positions. At Malplaquet Marlborough was again victorious, for he forced the French to retreat, but it was the bloodiest battle of the whole war and the losses of the Allies were far heavier than the French; over twenty thousand, compared with their ten or twelve thousand. 'A most murthering battle,' as Marlborough called it himself, and a carnage that was not seen in Europe again until the battle of Borodino. In Eng-

*'It is better
to contend with my
enemies than with
my own family'*

land Marlborough's enemies began to call him 'the butcher'.

For Anne the winter of 1708–9 had brought a more personal tragedy : the death of her beloved George. He had been seriously ill for several months, and she had spent many nights at Windsor and at Kensington holding him up in her arms to help him to breathe and imploring the doctors to find a cure. They did their horrifying best, with their cuppings, bleedings and blisterings, but, with or without their assistance, it was already clear by the summer of 1708 that Prince George was slowly dying, and only Anne clung fervently to the hope that anything could be done for him. In the autumn he recovered a little and they even planned a visit to the races at Newmarket, but then, on 23 October, he collapsed. On 28 October, with Anne at his bedside, he died.

It seems incredible that even at this moment, when Anne had just lost her constant companion of twenty-five years, Sarah could make herself unpleasant. But she could. News of the Prince's worsening condition had reached her while she was at Windsor Lodge, and at once she had driven to London, carrying with her a letter, not just offering Anne her sympathy but dredging up their own quarrels. Not surprisingly, Anne received her coolly. But Sarah was with her when George died, and tried to comfort her in the first paroxysms of grief, though she tactlessly referred to George's corpse as 'that dismal body'. Anne then asked to be by herself for a period, and then for Abigail to come in to her. Even now Sarah could not bring herself to pass on such a request, so that Abigail never got the message and Anne waited for her in vain. Sarah's dislike of her cousin had become completely obsessive and her description of the scene later that evening, as Anne finally prepared to leave for St James's, is without any trace of sympathy for the widowed Queen, but instead full of details about slights to herself and gestures to Abigail. As Anne left the Palace leaning on Sarah's arm, Abigail entered the gallery they were passing through, and Sarah recalled spitefully that Anne 'had strength enough to bend down towards Mrs Masham like a sail and in passing by went some steps more than was necessary to be nearer her, and when that cruel touch was over, of going by her with me, she turned about in a little passage-room and gave orders about her dogs and a strong-box'.

On 11 September 1709, the Duke of Marlborough and Prince Eugene defeated the French armies at Malplaquet, in one of the bloodiest battles of the century. The Allies lost more men than the French, and the Tories nicknamed Marlborough 'the butcher'.

But, whatever Sarah might say about the hardness of her feelings, Anne was heartbroken by George's death. She had lost the one companion from her childhood who had not failed her. Her father, sister, children, husband, were now all dead. She was acutely alone. All the family she now had was the young half-brother she did not know and who was claiming her Crown. The friendships of her youth, not just with Sarah but with Marlborough and Godolphin – 'we four who must never part' – had grown sour and stale and it was as a lonely widow that Anne faced the bleak remaining years ahead.

No royal consort until Victoria's Albert was mourned so elaborately or sincerely as George of Denmark. That winter Anne lived in almost total seclusion at St James's Palace, haunting the gloomy little closets where George used to make his model ships, overlooking the small sunless courtyard where Abigail hung the washing. Sarah, with her robust talent for survival, found such behaviour incomprehensibly morbid. 'I thought nothing was more natural than to avoid seeing of papers or anything that belonged to the one that one loved when they were just dead.'

Perhaps Anne drew some comfort from meticulously observing the correct precedents and etiquette for George's funeral and Court mourning. He was buried in November in Westminster Abbey 'after the same manner as Charles II, which was privately, at twelve at night'. Court mourning was made as elaborate as possible down to the smallest detail. Not only were the stairs at St James's draped with black flannel, but even the sconces on the wall were oxydised black. Only black pins on black pin-cushions were supplied to the palace, and peers were instructed that 'no person should use any varnished or bullion nails to be seen on their coaches, chariots or chairs'. When some ladies appeared at Court dressed in mourning but with coloured handkerchiefs, at once an order was given that no one with coloured handkerchiefs or anything coloured about them would be admitted to the Chapel Royal.

With unbelievable tactlessness, Parliament almost immediately passed an address suggesting that Anne should remarry, a proposal which, not surprisingly, deeply shocked her. The reply they received was unequivocal : 'The subject of this address is of such a nature that I am persuaded you do not expect a particular

'I am persuaded you do not expect a particular answer'

answer.' That the originator of the motion was a Whig was only what she expected of that party, even if this particular member of it was a half-wit. The relentless lords of the Junto were still pressing hard for Orford's appointment to the Privy Council, which they finally won in November: but as the year went on, with the Queen longing to get rid of them, and the war-weary country looking more and more to the Tories as the party of peace, it was becoming clear that they would not be able to remain in power for much longer.

But before the break came there were a few more scenes to be acted between Anne and Sarah. Sarah's official duties made her presence at Court unavoidable, but now each time there was a row over something. The question of lodgings cropped up, and Sarah accused Anne of giving to Abigail rooms she wanted herself to make a better entrance into her own apartments, and begrudging Marlborough 'a miserable hole to make a clear entry to his lodgings'. There was even a scene when Anne gave her sick laundress a bottle of wine a day without telling Sarah. Marlborough tried to restrain Sarah, warning her that 'all reproaches though ever so just, serve to no end but making the breach wider'. But weary of the war abroad and insecure at home, he, too, was beginning to lose his grip on events and to make mistakes on the political front, if not the battlefield. In October he unwisely asked the Queen to confirm his appointment as Captain-General for life. It was badly mistimed, flustered Anne and gave ammunition to his enemies. Abigail referred to him as 'King John' and others looked back to Cromwell's dictatorship and portrayed Marlborough as a similar rival to the Crown.

Such fears, if genuine, were unfounded, and Marlborough's wishes sprang not from overwhelming ambition but from fear that he would lose his position altogether if the Tories came back. The question returned again to Abigail's influence as the Tory mouthpiece at Court, and Anne felt obliged to write to Marlborough to deny that 'Masham' had advised her on the question – 'upon my word she knows nothing of it'. In 1710 Sunderland and other extreme Whigs wanted to raise the question of Abigail's influence in Parliament, but this was going too far for Godolphin's sense of decorum, and he stepped in to stop the plan going any further. But Marlborough, who had

THE
High Church Champion,
and his two seconds.

1709

'Tis these *False Brethren*, plague *ye* Church & State,
Princes dethrone, and *CIVIL WAR* create,
And the just power, of *Parliaments* debate.
Such pamper'd *Priests*, plead *ye Pretenders* cause
Support his *Faction* and despise the *Laws*
And cry *High Church*, is ruin'd and undone.
If *Persecution*, don't through *Britain* run.

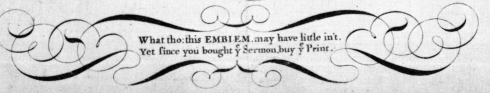

What tho: this EMBLEM, may have little in't.
Yet since you bought *ye* Sermon, buy *ye* Print.

retired to Windsor, was no longer attending Council meetings and Sunderland pressed him to deliver an ultimatum to Anne to choose between him and Abigail – 'a strange competition', as Sarah sourly commented to Anne, 'between one that has gained you so many battles and one that is but just worthy to brush your combs'. In the upshot Marlborough never faced Anne with a straight choice, and both he and Abigail stayed, but it was the Tories that came best out of the confrontation.

But far more dramatic and decisive in swinging the balance back to the Tories was the trial in February of Doctor Sacheverell. In November 1709 Sacheverell, an extreme High Churchman, had preached an incendiary Tory sermon at St Paul's before the City dignitaries, attacking Dissenters, toleration and the Revolution Settlement. Sacheverell had already aroused High Tory fever earlier in the reign, when at Oxford he had warned of the dire threat to the Church of England from Occasional Conformists, 'these crafty, faithless, and insidious persons who can creep to our altars and partake of our sacraments', as he described them. In 1702 he had launched the crusade against Dissenters in Parliament and had shown himself to be a powerful political force. Even so, had Godolphin and the Whigs taken no notice of his latest outburst, it could well have passed away without attracting very much attention. Their fatal mistake was to turn Sacheverell into a Tory martyr by deciding to impeach him.

The trial took place in Westminster Hall, still hung with the French standards captured at Blenheim. Wren was instructed to design special galleries to accommodate all the spectators, with special arrangements for a curtained box for Anne. Sacheverell's speech of defence was reported to have been written for him by the Tory propagandists, Swift and Atterbury, while the prosecutors were all Whigs. Thus the trial became not a question of proving Sacheverell's innocence or guilt, but of re-expounding the arguments of principle between the parties – the Church of England and Dissenters, the Revolution and hereditary right to the throne. Harley's wife who attended the trial, reported to her nephew that '... yesterday was taken up by the Doctor's counsel in reading passages ... full of the horridest blasphemy that was ever vented upon those called Christians; others full of base reflections upon the Queen and her family, one passage

OPPOSITE Doctor Sacheverell, the High Church Champion, with his two seconds, the Devil and the Pope. This print was circulated attacking Sacheverell after his High Tory sermon preached at St Paul's Cathedral in November 1709.

that she had no more title to the Crown than my Lord Mayor's horse …'.

But the country at large was for Sacheverell and against the Whigs. Each day, as Sacheverell was driven from the Temple where he was lodged, to Westminster, his coach was surrounded by cheering crowds. A brisk trade was conducted in prints of his head, and any misguided person who failed to show sufficient enthusiasm on his behalf was severely dealt with. One man in London had his skull cleft, simply for not joining in the cheers as Sacheverell's coach drove by. Mobs attacked the houses of several prominent Whigs, and in Lincoln's Inn a Presbyterian Meeting House was destroyed and a bonfire made of the pulpit.

Anne attended the trial every day during the three weeks it lasted. It was assumed that she must be for Sacheverell against the Whigs, but she gave no public indication of her sympathies. 'God bless Your Majesty and the Church! We hope Your Majesty is for Doctor Sacheverell,' cried the crowd as her coach rumbled along the streets to Westminster. In private she told Burnet that it was a bad sermon and Sacheverell deserved to be punished. He was far too much of an extremist for her liking, though she can hardly have regretted the unpopularity of the Whigs.

Sacheverell was finally voted guilty by sixty-nine votes to fifty-two, but his sentence – a three-year suspension from preaching and the burning of the offending sermon before the Royal Exchange – was such a lenient one that it was widely hailed as a Tory victory.

Sarah, as a Whig, was naturally upset at a time when her whole attitude towards Anne was becoming even more embittered. During the trial she had, characteristically, quarrelled not about the issues involved but about whether Anne wanted her ladies to sit or stand. It seemed a trivial matter but Sarah was consumed by the suspicion that the Duchess of Somerset (who stood when Sarah sat) wanted to oust her from the Court offices, and created a scene. After the trial her behaviour deteriorated further and it was reported to Anne that Sarah had called her 'a praying godly idiot'. Anne's patience was running out. When in April Sarah requested an audience, Anne did her best to avoid it, asking her to write instead, and saying she would be

Painted fan celebrating the happy outcome of the trial of Doctor Sacheverell for the Church of England and the Queen. The eye of Providence looks down upon St Paul's Cathedral, representing the Anglican Church, and the Queen, while six bishops surround the Doctor.

unable to receive her until after Easter. Undeterred, on the Thursday before Easter, Sarah arrived at Kensington. It was to be the last time they ever saw each other.

Unfortunately the only account of what went on comes from Sarah, and we can only try to read between the lines. Sarah maintained she tried to clear herself of 'some particular calumnies with which I had been loaded', but Anne refused to be drawn into an argument, kept repeating that Sarah should go away and put anything she wanted to say into writing, and that she would give her no answer at that moment. Sarah suspected that Anne had been briefed, but the fear of emotional scenes and the obstinate refusal to enter into any discussion are characteristic of her. And her decision, after all the scenes, tears, rudeness and gossip, that she would never receive Sarah again, was not, whatever Sarah might say, anything except reasonable in the circumstances. But it was a squalid ending to one of the most celebrated friendships in English history.

Even after the final separation, the quarrel spluttered on in an undignified way until early in 1711. Angry letters passed to and fro when Swift, used by Harley to attack the Whigs in the Press, launched an attack on the Marlboroughs' finances and accused Sarah of peculating £22,000. She demanded a vindication from the Queen, and got it. 'Everybody knows,' said Anne, 'cheating is not the Duchess of Marlborough's fault.' Then Sarah, stung by Swift's onslaught, got hold of the idea of publishing some of Anne's letters to her in revenge – an unpleasant thought for a Queen who hated the idea of being made a laughing-stock, and the subject of gossip. There was some anxious to-ing and fro-ing by intermediaries to try to prevent Sarah, but though she never, in fact, carried out her threat, she hung on to the letters.

She refused, too, to relinquish her Court appointments though, as she never now went near Anne, she could not perform her duties. The situation was a ridiculous one and in January 1711, when Marlborough was back in England, Anne demanded from him that Sarah should return her golden key of office within three days. On his knees he pleaded for his wife, but Anne, muttering something inaudible about her honour, insisted, and refused to discuss any other business with him. When Marlborough returned to Sarah to tell her he had failed, she flung the key on the floor at his feet.

By the time Sarah was dismissed, the expected changes in the ministry had already taken place. The first new appointment was that of the moderate and much respected Duke of Shrewsbury – whom Harley had been cultivating assiduously – to the post of Lord Chamberlain, in place of the Earl of Kent, soon after Sacheverell's trial. Kent was a very secondary figure – the only one of Anne's Lord Chamberlains who was not a member of the Cabinet and who was known contemptuously as 'the Bug' because, even by eighteenth-century standards, he smelled. No one except The Bug himself objected to his dismissal, but not only was Shrewsbury now counted a Tory, but Anne had made the appointment without consulting Godolphin, who was at Newmarket. He was dismayed when he heard the news and took up his pen immediately to warn her that '... Your Majesty is suffering yourself to be guided to your own ruin and destruction as fast as it is possible for them to compass it to whom you seem so much to hearken'.

174

Sunderland was the next, and the first of the Junto, to fall. Anne had detested him for years and in June she wrote to inform (not to consult) Godolphin and to forestall any objection about the damage it might do to Marlborough's credit abroad :

> It is true indeed that turning a son-in-law out of his office may be a mortification to the Duke of Marlborough, but must the fate of Europe depend on that, and must he be gratified in all his desires, and I not in so reasonable a thing as parting with a man whom I took into my service with all the uneasiness imaginable, and whose behaviour to me has been so ever since and who, I must add, is obnoxious to all people except a few.

But no change could be complete while Godolphin remained in office and Harley out of it. Anne hesitated a long while before dismissing Godolphin. Though in his old age he had grown crotchety, and their personal relationship had never been a very close one, he had served her right from the beginning of the reign and had gained such a reputation that it was hard to imagine the future without him. She had been warned of the effect it would have on England's credit abroad, and on the price of stocks in the City. The directors of the Bank of England had come in a deputation to warn her of the financial crises that would ensue. Godolphin's letter of dismissal was written early in July, but was not sent until early August. Anne was being pushed by Harley, but in her delays she showed herself as devious as he was, telling Godolphin to his face she was going to keep him on the very day before she sent the letter. There was no farewell interview : 'I desire that instead of bringing the staff to me you will break it, which I believe will be easier to both of us.' The pension she promised him of £4,000 a year was never paid, and he ended his life dependent on the charity of his brother. When he died two years later, Sarah wrote in her Bible, 'Today died the best man that ever lived.' He was certainly the greatest statesman of the age, and Anne's treatment of him was the meanest gesture she ever made as Queen.

With Godolphin gone, the Tory triumph seemed complete. Harley replaced Godolphin at the head of Anne's government, though as Chancellor of the Exchequer, not Lord Treasurer, and the old figures streamed back into office – Rochester, Buckingham and St John. In October a general election return-

'Today died the best man that ever lived'

ed the Tory Parliament Harley needed, and the Whigs were in full retreat.

But if the Tories were the peace party, they had yet to obtain the terms of a settlement that would bring it about. And as Anne grew older and goutier they had, too, to bring themselves to face the question of the succession, not as a distant contingency, but as an increasingly pressing problem.

7
Tory Peace and Whig Succession 1711-14

IN FEBRUARY 1711 Anne celebrated her forty-sixth birthday at St James's Palace. For the occasion she wore a gown of green flowered satin embroidered with gold, and attended a special performance of 'an Italian dialogue in Her Majesty's praise set to excellent music by the famous Mr Handel, a retainer to the Court of Hanover in the quality of Director of His Electoral Highness's Chapel ... and sung by Grimaldi and other celebrated voices of the Italian opera with which Her Majesty was extremely well pleased'. Reflecting the political changes of the previous year, the entertainment was an almost exclusively Tory affair and most of the Whigs boycotted the Palace. The Tory ladies, however, put on a good show, some 'scarce able to move under the load of jewels', and it was said that such a splendid Court had not been seen since 1660.

Outward display, however, could not hide from those around her that the Queen, ageing prematurely and rapidly, was growing not only infirm but incapable. Her chief doctor and close friend, Sir David Hamilton, felt compelled to warn her of the dangers of her 'disquiets and uneasiness', while her ministers, needing decisions, met only with prevarication. Harley found that there was 'no other remedy but to let Her Majesty take her own time which never failed to be the very longest that the nature of the thing would suffer her to defer it'. Swift described her as : 'extremely cautious and slow and after the usual mistake of those who think they have been often imposed on, became so very suspicious that she overshot the mark and erred in the other extreme'. It was hardly a happy auspice under which Anne once more confronted the rounds of party struggle, personal dilemma and the issues of war and peace.

The new Tory ministers, triumphant at the polls, were quickly disillusioned with the Queen. Their plans to press ahead with the old Church bills against Dissenters foundered on Anne's obstinacy. 'I have changed my ministers,' she declared, 'but I have not changed my measures ; I am still for moderation and will govern by it.' The Tories discovered that in practice this meant that not only did she frown on their High Church zeal, but that a number of moderate Whigs, including the Duke of Somerset, still kept their places in the ministry. Tory discontent began to voice itself through the October Club, so called because 'the strongest ale is brewed in the month of

'I have changed my ministers, but I have not changed my measures'

October', and Swift described how they 'meet every evening at a tavern near Parliament to consult affairs and to drive things on to extremes against the Whigs ... the Ministry is for gentler measures and the other Tories for more violent'. Harley complained, 'the Queen, sensible how much she was governed by the late Ministry, runs a little into t'other extreme and is jealous in that point even of those that have got her out of the others' hands'.

Harley, nevertheless, was the lynch-pin of this government, and the man on whom Anne depended in her declining years. It was thus with anguish that she learned, in March, of an attempt on her minister's life which very nearly succeeded. On the anniversary of the Queen's accession, 8 March, there was another Court festival at St James's, for which Harley dressed elaborately in a thick embroidered waistcoat with gold brocade flowers on a background of silver and blue – clothes which had originally been made for the Queen's birthday celebrations the month before, but which his careful wife had decided could, with the addition of a silver fringe, quite well serve a second time. On his way to St James's he caught sight of a Frenchman called de Guiscard, a disreputable character who had first deserted France to spy for England, but whom Harley knew to be acting as a double agent. And so, after presenting his compliments to the Queen, Harley returned to his office where he issued a warrant for the Frenchman's arrest, and also arranged a meeting of the leading ministers to interrogate him at the Cockpit that afternoon. There, after a prolonged cross-examination, de Guiscard suddenly took a knife from his pocket and lunged at the minister. At once there was total confusion, as the other councillors drew their swords and rushed in to beat off the would-be assassin. St John, shouting 'the villain has killed Mr Harley', broke his sword before de Guiscard, badly wounded, was overcome and dragged away. Harley, though bleeding profusely and very weak, was not dead. By an amazing stroke of fortune the knife had struck one of the gold flowers of his waistcoat, breaking the force of a thrust which otherwise could have killed him.

When Anne was told of the attempted assassination, her first thought was that Harley's death was being kept from her. Even when she was convinced he would recover, she remained

distracted, wept for two hours, could not sleep for several nights and, to the distress of her doctors, worked herself into a fever. Among her attendants it was recalled with horror that only a few days previously de Guiscard had been given an audience at Court, and had been left quite alone with Anne except for a lady-in-waiting, and no one else within call 'but Mrs Kirk who was commonly asleep'. It might well, her ladies told each other, have been a fatal attack on Anne herself, not a pen-knife attempt on Harley. After the de Guiscard affair, the locks at Kensington were changed and the guard doubled, though it would never, at any stage, have been difficult to assassinate Anne.

Politically de Guiscard's attack brought contradictory results. In the country at large the convalescent Harley never enjoyed such popularity. But at Court his absence opened the door to his most dangerous political rival, Henry St John. St John had risen in Harley's wake, but, though a man of wit and charm and probably the most eloquent speaker in the Commons, he was also ambitious, rash and unstable. He had begun his political career as a Tory 'high-flier' and in 1702 had vigorously support-ed the Occasional Conformity Bill. He had split with the extremists in his party over the issue of voting supplies for the war, and, as we have seen, had entered the reformed ministry of 1704 as Secretary at War. But now, in 1711, he was once more strengthening his links with the extremists and voicing their discontent against Harley's cautious moderation. Accord-ing to Harley's own testimony, it was in February that 'there began a separation in the House of Commons and Mr Secretary St John began listing a party', and in the same month St John ceased to invite him to his house in Golden Square. Harley's absence from London seemed a heaven-sent opportunity for St John to further his own interests.

So far, St John's main recommendation to Anne had been that he was a protégé of Harley. She was not impervious to his charm, but the stories she had heard of his private life – how he neglected his wife and spent his leisure in the company of prostitutes and drunkards – was hardly a passport to her favour, and she distrusted his flamboyance and instability. Even so, he was still her Secretary of State and an able and energetic one, and even if she had wanted to, she was quite unable to hold him down in Harley's absence.

OPPOSITE Henry St John, Viscount Bolingbroke: portrait painted by A. S. Belle after Bolingbroke's flight to France in 1715. In 1711 Bolingbroke began to supervise the secret negotiations with the French, and to challenge Harley's position as Anne's chief minister and leader of the Tories.

In 1712, while the secret negotiations between the British and the French were still at a delicate stage, the British commander, Ormonde, was under orders not to engage the enemy in battle. The Allies were kept in ignorance of this arrangement but inevitably their suspicions were aroused. This print shows a Dutch satire on the 'secret' negotiations.

It was with the peace negotiations that St John made his most successful bid for power. Harley had started secret negotiations in August 1710, using as go-between a French cleric, a former chaplain to the captured Marshal Tallard, called Abbé Gaultier. In January 1711 Gaultier was smuggled through the English lines to Paris to meet Louis's Foreign Minister, de Torcy. At first only Harley and the Duke of Shrewsbury knew of the negotiations and then, a month or so later, Anne was informed, but the Secretaries of State and the rest of the Cabinet were all kept in the dark. But in the spring of 1711, as rumours about the negotiations were beginning to leak out anyway, St John stepped in during Harley's absence to handle them.

There were good reasons for keeping the negotiations secret. Although the country was sick of the war, and the Tories were protesting loudly against voting supplies – 'to give six millions with so little fruit,' wailed one back-bencher in 1711, 'Lord have mercy upon us, what bubbles do our Allies make of us!' – the Whigs were certain to oppose the type of settlement proposed. While they were still sticking to their cry of 'No peace without Spain!' the Tories were heartily sick of pursuing this ever-receding goal, and the unexpected accession of the Archduke Charles to the Austrian Empire on the death of his elder brother in 1711, lent further weight to their views, for the Tories could now argue that the combination of Spain with the vast Habsburg lands in central Europe would be just as threatening to the balance of European power as the Bourbon alliance between Spain and France. And, in fact, by the time St John took over the peace negotiations, it had already been secretly agreed with France that Philip should keep Spain and that Charles should have just the Spanish lands in Italy and the Netherlands. But the manner of making peace as well as the contents of the treaty was a party issue. Any separately-negotiated treaty between Britain and France was bound to be denounced by the Whigs as a fundamental breach of the terms of the Grand Alliance, and as a treacherous betrayal of the Allies; while to the Tories, who had never felt any great loyalty to the other members of the Alliance, a separately-negotiated peace was both the quickest method of producing a settlement and the best way to obtain favourable terms for Britain. Throughout the summer and early

England's American colonies flourished during Anne's time. It has been estimated that the population of the British settlements on the mainland of America rose from about 200,000 in the year of the Glorious Revolution to nearly 350,000 at the time of the Treaty of Utrecht. This lithograph shows the Stadt Huys of New York in 1679.

The East India Company

It was the trade with India and the East that most captured men's imagination in the early eighteenth century. Many of Queen Anne's subjects braved the terrible Indian climate to seek their fortunes in the service of the great East India Company, while at home fashionable society provided an eager market for exotic imports like tea, silk, china and lacquerwork.

RIGHT East India House in Leadenhall Street, from an engraving by George Vertue in 1711. This house had been built at the end of the sixteenth century as a town house for Sir William Craven, but was leased to the Company as their first London headquarters.

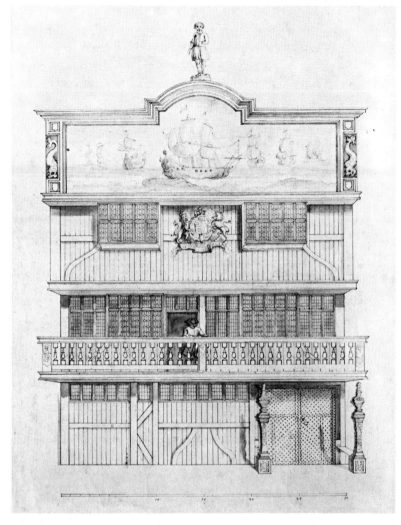

RIGHT AND FAR RIGHT Illustrations from the log-book kept by a Company employee, describing his voyage out to India in 1688.

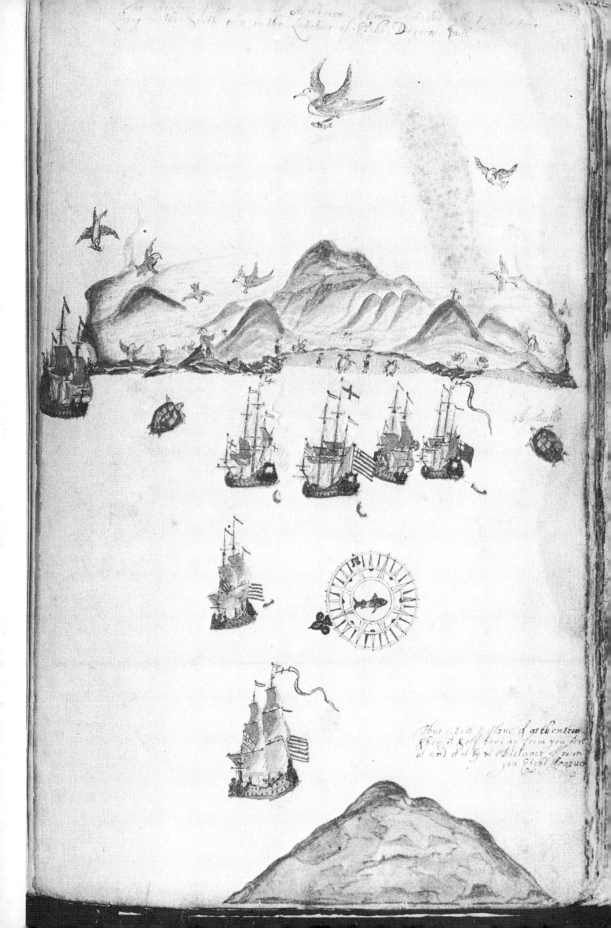

autumn of 1711, St John negotiated tirelessly with de Torcy. Though he was the leader of the back-bench Tories in their resentment against the moneyed Whig interest, his vision was far greater than theirs, for he had realised that England's future lay on the seas, in trade and commerce, and was determined that Britain's gains in the peace settlement should provide her with a solid basis from which to further her world-wide trade. The points he set out to win from France included the Asiento, a monopoly of the Spanish-American slave trade; Gibraltar and Port Mahon as permanent bases in the Mediterranean; Acadia and Newfoundland in North America, with the restoration of the Hudson Bay Company's territories and forts; and, nearer home, the destruction of the fortifications of Dunkirk, which for years had been the basis for the French privateers who had attacked and harassed vessels sailing in the English Channel. De Torcy's first reaction was that the English were demanding 'such considerable advantages as must absolutely ruin all commerce but their own' but, in the long run, after months of patient haggling, St John got what he wanted and thereby laid the basis for Britain's great era of trading and maritime supremacy for the next two centuries. Even when Harley returned to London in May – to be welcomed by Anne with his elevation to Earl of Oxford and Mortimer – St John continued as the driving force behind the negotiations.

But as the news of the negotiations spread, the Whigs were preparing for a fight. When the negotiations were laid before Parliament, the Whigs made 'all the noise and bustle they could against the peace'. Harley did his best to make counter-preparations, playing for time by proroguing the opening of Parliament until early December, and exhorting all Tories to attend the session. Although Harley's whips worked diligently, it was Swift's propaganda that provided his most effective weapon. In November Swift published a devastating pamplet entitled *The Conduct of the Allies*, which ran through five editions before the end of the year – 'a prodigious run', the author exclaimed delightedly, '... considering 'tis a dear twelvepenny book'. But it struck precisely the right note for the Tory cause. The prolongation of the war was depicted as a conspiracy among the Allies, connived at by the Whigs. All along, argued Swift, England had borne the brunt of the struggle while the Dutch

Daniel Finch, 2nd Earl of
Nottingham: portrait
attributed to Richardson.

had refused to risk their troops in battle, the Austrians had not
even provided troops to risk, and as for the failings of the
Portuguese, they were almost, but not quite, past description.

Anne's speech opening Parliament, prepared for her by
Harley, was further anti-Whig propaganda. 'I am glad that I can
now tell you that notwithstanding the arts of those who delight
in war, both time and place are appointed for opening the treaty
of a general peace.' The Whigs were indignant at such a Tory
blast from the throne and even the old Whig courtier, Lord
Cowper, ruefully complained that the Queen should not 'have
thundered in such a way'. Yet when Anne disrobed and returned to listen to the debate *incognito*, she found the Whigs quite
undeterred in voicing their opposition and the debate a furious
one. Moreover, the Whigs had, in the weeks before the session,
struck a bargain with Nottingham by which, in return for their
votes in support of his Occasional Conformity Bill, Nottingham agreed to oppose the ministry over the peace. On the Whig

189

side it was bare-faced cynicism and a complete betrayal of their principles on religious toleration, but as a Parliamentary manœuvre it was highly effective. After Anne's speech, Nottingham rose to deliver a passionate hour-long harangue 'that no peace could be safe or honourable to Great Britain or to Europe, if Spain and the West Indies were allotted to any branch of the House of Bourbon'. Lord Anglesea retorted with a censure on the Duke of Marlborough, saying that 'the country might have enjoyed the blessings of peace soon after the battle of Ramillies if it had not been deferred by some persons whose interest it was to prolong the war'. At this, Marlborough sprang indignantly to his feet and appealed directly to the embarrassed Queen (who officially was not present) to exonerate him. When the votes were finally counted, it was realised that the government had been defeated, and its very existence seemed in jeopardy.

But it was not beaten yet. If the peace had been thrown out by the Lords, then the answer was to create enough new Tory peers to ensure its support. A list of twelve names was drawn up, and though Anne disliked the idea, she admitted that 'no body could propose a better expedient'. The fact that one of the new peers was Samuel Masham, Abigail's husband, was no recommendation of the scheme. 'I never had the least intention of making a great lady of Abigail Masham,' Anne protested, 'for by so doing I should lose a useful servant about my person for it would give offence for a peeress to lie on the floor and do all sorts of inferior offices.' It was only on the condition that Abigail 'remained a dresser and did as she used to do' that Masham got his coronet.

In the House of Lords the arrival of the new peers caused an outburst of protest and the Whig wits quickly set to work. Wharton rose to enquire whether 'they intended to vote as individuals or according to their Foreman'. The story was put about too that when Harley's pious wife made some mention of 'the Lord Jehovah', Shrewsbury's Italian Countess assumed she must be referring to one of the new peers as 'she had never heard the name before'. But for the ministry the device saved the day and the Whigs were obliged to admit defeat.

The Tories drove home their advantage by attacking Marlborough. They had already run a Press campaign against him, dismissing his victories at Blenheim as a 'stroke of fortune' and describing the capture of Bouchain in his most recent campaign as 'the capture of a dove-cote'. With the peace preliminaries settled, they had no more use for him and moved in for the kill. Before the year ended Anne sent him a letter of dismissal. What it said we do not know, for in a rare burst of temper the Duke threw it into the fire. But he replied to her with his customary dignity and politeness:

> I am very sensible of the honour Your Majesty does me in dismissing me from your service by a letter of your own hand, though I find by it that my enemies have been able to prevail with Your Majesty to do it in the manner that is most injurious to me. ... I wish Your Majesty may never find the want of so faithful a servant as I have always endeavoured to approve myself to you.

While in the House of Commons charges were being prepared against him for peculation and misappropriation of public funds, it was left to Louis XIV to pay the closing tribute to Marlborough's military career: 'the affair of displacing the Duke of Marlborough will do all for us we desire'. When, late in 1712, Marlborough decided to leave England and live abroad for a time, Anne refused even to grant him a farewell audience. Sarah had deserved her dismissal, but Marlborough was the outstanding figure of her reign who had served her faithfully. The friendship and service of over twenty years could not have ended on a sourer note.

It was, indeed, the end of an era, and Anne's private thoughts as she watched her great servant depart may well have dwelled in areas very different from those mirrored by her stern public face. The friendships of her youth were disappearing as she herself was entering her premature dotage. She had found nothing to replace the companionship of the now-remote Sarah. Abigail, low-born and self-seeking, had passed the peak of such influence as she had; the aristocratic Duchess of Somerset was indeed a friend, but never an intimate one. As the Queen entered her lonely old age so, naturally but woundingly, men looked beyond the present reign to the next one – as one Tory Member of Parliament put it, 'the circumstance that sits heaviest upon the hearts of all thinking and serious men'. At no time was the Hanoverian succession a foregone conclusion and, during Anne's last years, the Jacobites in England were more active

'The affair of displacing the Duke of Marlborough will do all for us we desire'

than at any other time during the reign. Every time Anne fell ill the coffee houses buzzed with rumours that the Pretender had been informed and was preparing to set sail to claim his inheritance.

No issue divided the Tories like the issue of the succession, and, as it grew more urgent, it came to dominate political life, making all other issues appear transient and secondary. While the Whigs were united in their support for Hanover, the Tory party covered every shade of opinion, from uncompromising Jacobites to men who were as staunchly for Hanover as any Whig, and there was little sympathy between the two extremes. But nothing was so discouraging to the Hanoverian Tories as the alliance between George of Hanover and the Whigs. In the controversy over the peace he had come out strongly against the Tories, and with stories of Tory Jacobitism being fed to him by the Whigs, it was growing clear that the Hanoverian succession would end the Tories' supremacy. In this confused situation, as in the first years after 1688, prudent men attempted to insure their positions against either possible outcome. On the Continent, Marlborough carried this policy to its most successful height, and gained for himself both a pardon from the Pretender and the promise from Hanover that he would be put in charge of the troops to repel any Jacobite invasion. But in England the Queen's ministers, too, were plotting and bluffing. Even Harley, keeping it quiet from Anne, was trying to ingratiate himself with Hanover, but the French had not yet despaired of his coming out for the Pretender. As for the rash St John, now created Viscount Bolingbroke, his Jacobite intrigues were the talk of the town, and on the Continent at any rate there was no doubt about his intentions. In the summer of 1712, furious because Anne had created him only a Viscount and not an Earl like Harley, Bolingbroke was sent to Paris to finalise the peace terms in an attempt to assuage his wounded pride, but ended by infuriating Anne. Not only did he take an ex-nun for his mistress, but he attended the same performance of the opera as the Pretender, and did not, as the Queen thought he should have done, immediately leave the theatre.

Anne's own attitude to the succession was contributing to the insecurity and rumours. In this final, long drawn-out crisis of her reign she became adept at dissembling and concealing her

Riots in Bloomsbury in 1712, which broke out as a result of quarrels between Low Church supporters, encouraged by Whig fanatics, and drinkers of toasts to the Queen.

thoughts, and on this, the most sensitive subject of all, until the very end, she took no one into her confidence. In Parliament she publicly acknowledged the Hanoverian succession, but this was not sufficient to scotch the rumours. Anne's dislike of the Hanoverians was well known and she still refused to tolerate the idea that George or one of his family should come over to secure the succession. There were stories that she had changed her mind and would invite her half-brother to share her throne, that she had left a will contravening the Act, and that the Jacobites were mustering their strength for a show-down. The question of the Pretender's future had inevitably come up in the peace negotiations with France, and in 1712 Anne received a long letter from James 'to compose our differences'. He reminded her of their father 'who loved you tenderly' and asked her '… to prefer your own brother, the last male of our name, to the duchess of Hanover, the remotest relation we have, whose friendship you have no reason to rely on, or to be fond of, and who will leave the government to foreigners of another language'. He received no reply.

Amid the flying rumours and growing insecurity, Anne's health was giving way. In 1713 she did not walk at all from January to July, and was too ill to attend the celebrations for the signing of the Treaty of Utrecht in the summer. In December she caught a fever and lay for several hours unconscious, while rumours that she was already dead and the Pretender about to set sail with a squadron of French men-of-war, plunged the City into panic, which Harley tried to check by driving leisurely round the parks to show he thought all was well. She survived, but never properly recovered. Her face was quite altered and discoloured, and henceforth whenever she made a public appearance, she was heavily made up to conceal the change. 'She did not look like the same person as before and therefore 'twas expedient to use paint to disguise the discolourings; but this was kept so secret that it never was as much as whispered in her lifetime,' ran one account.

Meanwhile, when his wisdom was most needed, Harley was clearly losing his grip. The tireless, scheming politician of earlier years was growing apathetic. Never a clear speaker, even in his prime, he was now becoming virtually unintelligible. An emissary from Hanover reported back to George that 'I am assured from all hands, especially by those who had business to transact with the Treasurer, that it is impossible to comprehend the answers he gives, much less put them afterwards in writing. Besides, he frequently gives such as have no connexion with the proposals which were made to him.' So marked was the deterioration that Anne, too, found him difficult to deal with and was eventually compelled to issue a rebuke : 'Now that I have a pen in my hand,' she wrote, 'I cannot help desiring you again when you come next to speak plainly, lay everything open, or else how is it possible I can judge of anything.'

In March Anne was carried to the House of Lords to open Parliament and declared in her speech that all 'attempts to weaken my authority or to render the possession of the crown uneasy to me can never be proper means to strengthen the succession'. But her message to Parliament seemed to be offset in April by her unwillingness to agree to setting a price on the Pretender's head. 'I do not at this time see any occasion for such a proclamation,' she stated sharply, and when Sophia sent a message to England enquiring whether her grandson (the future George II), in his capacity as Duke of Cambridge, might receive a writ summoning him to the House of Lords, Anne was furious. Harley said he had never seen her so angry before. She certainly shocked him into acting swiftly to prevent the Prince coming over, though Bolingbroke and Abigail tried to insinuate that the whole affair had been contrived by Harley to start with. When Anne wrote to Hanover in May her tone was stinging. 'Nothing,' she informed George, 'could be more dangerous to the tranquility of my estates, to the right of succession in your line, nor consequently more disagreeable to me at this juncture than such a demarche.' Her coldness greatly depressed the Electress Sophia, who gave orders for two of Anne's letters to be printed so that 'the world might see it was not her fault if her children lost three kingdoms'. Though thirty years Anne's senior, Sophia by now was expected to outlive her and to become the first of the Hanoverian monarchs of Great Britain. She very nearly did so, but on 8 June, while walking in her gardens, she suddenly collapsed and died. Some said it was Anne who was responsible for having 'cast such a damp upon her spirits', but Anne showed no sign of remorse, or even of sorrow. Sophia's death, she informed David Hamilton,

'It was not
her fault if her
children lost three
kingdoms'

was 'chipping porridge' to her and she was quite indifferent to the news.

Anne herself had little more than two months left to live, but her last days were as troubled as any before. The quarrel between Harley and Bolingbroke was coming to a head. Harley accused Bolingbroke of peculation, and each was openly trying to over-throw the other. Anne implored the Duke of Shrewsbury to try to bring about a reconciliation, but it was a hopeless task. Bolingbroke's financial dishonesty nearly threatened to be his downfall, and in July he, with Abigail in his wake, was accused of having illegally profited from the Asiento slave contract under the Treaty of Utrecht. There was talk of a public enquiry, even impeachment, when Anne stepped in to dampen the crisis by proroguing Parliament.

With her ministry split down the middle, and virtually no one whom she could trust, Anne, after delaying and dissembling for months, suddenly came down finally on the side of Hanover. Her ministers she had lost faith in, but her doctors were her confidants, and in an interview with David Hamilton on 27 July, Anne asked him to go secretly to Hanover as her personal envoy and to assure George of her friendship. Even the dreaded prospect of George's coming to England in Anne's own life-time was to be suggested and welcomed.

The same day Anne dismissed Harley from her service. The reasons she gave were that he 'neglected all business; that he was seldom to be understood; that when he did explain himself she could not depend upon the truth of what he said; that he never came to her at the time she appointed; that he often came drunk; that lastly, to crown all, he behaved himself towards her with ill manner, indecency and disrespect'. That evening Harley attended a Council meeting, and in front of Anne hurled a salvo of accusations at Bolingbroke, ranging from peculation to high treason. The meeting lasted until two in the morning, and Anne found the scenes almost beyond endurance. In a mood of despair and of prophecy she told Arbuthnot that she doubted if she would be able to last much longer.

8 Anne's England 1714

THE NEXT DAY, Wednesday, Anne lost her appetite and was very low-spirited. She again attended a meeting of her Council, but appeared withdrawn and said little. Early the following morning her doctors were summoned and found her with 'a trembling in her hands, a pain and heat in her head with sleepiness ... and a little bleeding at the nose'. After some debate among themselves they decided to cup her to give her some relief, and she was able to sleep again until seven o'clock. Then,

> ... finding herself pretty well [she] rose from the bed and got her hair combed. This done, towards eight Her Majesty went to look on the clock, and Mrs Danvers taking notice that she fixed her eyes a long time upon it, asked Her Majesty what she saw in the clock more than ordinary. The Queen answered her only with turning her head and a dying look at which Mrs Danvers being frightened she called for help.

Her physician again rushed to her room and let her blood after which, not altogether surprisingly, she became unconscious for about an hour. When she revived, the Duchess of Somerset asked her how she was, to which the Queen replied, 'Never worse. I am going.'

But Anne was not to be allowed to die in peace. The Privy Councillors in session at the Cockpit were summoned to Kensington, and Anne was confronted with one more great issue of State. As Harley had been dismissed, the crucial office of Lord Treasurer was vacant, and everyone was anxious to avoid Anne dying without leaving anyone at the head of the government, before George arrived from Hanover. The Jacobites, of course, hoped that Bolingbroke would succeed his old rival, but his hour had passed. His appointment could well have led the country into civil war, and when they arrived at Kensington the Privy Councillors had already decided to recommend the Duke of Shrewsbury. How much the dying Queen understood of what was going on is impossible to say, but she managed to muster her strength to place the Treasurer's Staff of Office into the Duke's hands. The effect on the Jacobites, according to Defoe was 'like a clap of Christmas thunder to a female soothsayer'. While they remained an ill-concerted group with no clear direction, the Privy Councillors took rapid steps to safe-

PREVIOUS PAGES A view across the Thames, looking towards the Temple. The sterns of the two barges are decorated with the Queen's cipher. Painting by an unknown artist, 1703.

Charles Talbot, Duke of
Shrewsbury, who was
made Lord Treasurer by
the Queen on her
death-bed. Portrait by
Godfrey Kneller, *c.* 1685.

guard the country against an invasion by the Pretender. The
trained bands were mustered, troops brought over from
Flanders and the coastal defences put in readiness. After
only a day or so, it was clear that an invasion would, as Bolingbroke told the Pretender later, have been in 'the last degree
extravagant'.

While her country prepared for her successor, Anne's doctors
were desperately trying every horrific remedy they knew. Not
only was she bled again, but hot irons were applied to blister
her skin, she was given cardis to make her vomit, her feet
were covered with garlic and, the final indignity, her head was
shaved quite bare. It was all a public spectacle too, for her room
was crowded with attendants. Apart from seven doctors, there

199

were her ladies and at least three clergymen ready to administer the last rites of the Church. From Kensington premature rumours of her death were reaching the capital. On Saturday, 31 July, Swift received a letter from one of the gentlemen at Court telling him how 'a report was carried to town that she was actually dead. She was not prayed for even at her own chapel at St James's, and what is more infamous, stocks arose three per cent upon it in the City'.

But, though on the 31st Anne was still alive, she was in a coma and sinking fast. 'Last night,' continues the report, 'the Speaker and my Lord Chief Justice Parker were sent for ... This morning the Hanover envoy was ordered to attend with the black box [nominating thirteen Lord Justices as regents], and the heralds to be in readiness to proclaim the new King. ...' They had not long to wait. On the morning of Sunday, 1 August, Queen Anne died at 7.30. 'I believe,' wrote Arbuthnot, 'sleep was never more welcome to a weary traveller than death was to her.'

Among Anne's papers a draft, unsigned will was found, but there was nothing in it to alarm the Regents. There was a request to be buried beside her husband, provision for her servants and a bequest of £2,000 'to the poor', but no mention of the name of her successor. A hunt was started for a signed will, which many believed to exist. 'For a long time past,' runs an account in the Stuart papers, 'she always carried about her and put every evening under a bolster a sealed packet of which she changed the envelope when it got dirty or worn, which was suspected to be a will concerning the Pretender.' If it did exist, which is unlikely, the will was never found, but the Regents did discover a bundle of papers 'the thickness of four fingers, sealed with her Majesty's seal and written on the outside in her own hand that she desired these papers should be burnt'. Tantalisingly, her wish was respected and the bundle was thrown onto a fire, but the Hanoverian envoy who was present thought that, as the papers fell apart, he glimpsed the handwriting of the Pretender.

But the Hanoverian succession was now in no danger. Under Shrewsbury's calm guidance, the provision of the Act of Settlement came into operation so smoothly that the fears and panics of the past months seemed almost a false alarm. 'Everything is in tranquility,' ran one contemporary account, 'and the stocks rise upon the bettering of the times.' While the Jacobites in England and abroad waited in vain for guidance, in Hanover, George, reassured by comforting reports from England, was in no hurry to take possession of his new inheritance. He did not finally arrive in England until the middle of September, over a month after Anne's death.

And so the House of Stuart gave way to the House of Hanover; an English sovereign to a German; an era of war to a new age of peace. In most respects Anne's death itself was of little consequence. The great issues of history are rarely shaped by the birth and death of monarchs, and certainly the passing of the passive Anne marked no sharp watershed in the nation's development. Even the personalities who dominated in the new reign were inherited from the old: among the Whigs, the old lords of the Junto had already begun to slip away in the final months of Anne's reign, to be replaced by younger men like Sunderland and Walpole, who were both to reach the peak of their influence under George I. Yet for some individuals Anne's death did mark a final eclipse. Sarah, of course, and Abigail, had no role to play in the new régime. Abigail died in 1734, a rich woman who had successfully plundered the secret service funds in the last months before Anne's death to provide for her obscurity under the new dynasty. Sarah survived until 1744, quarrelling with everyone from her servants to her grandchildren, but politically impotent and living on her memories of past glory. Anne's great Duke faded rapidly into old age, travelling from one health spa to the next, until his death at Blenheim Palace seven years after that of his Queen. For the Tory party as a whole, the new dynasty brought virtual elimination. Harley was never again to hold public office, found himself impeached by the rabid Whig Commons and languished for two years in the Tower before his release in 1717, a broken man. Bolingbroke fled into exile and there exercised himself in the wild fantasies of a Jacobite Restoration, participating in 1715, in the failure of the first Jacobite rising. His subsequent career passed from failure to impotence, such impotence, in fact, that after he quarrelled with the Stuart Pretender, King George saw no reason to withhold a pardon and he lived his last days in obscurity, but at home, consoling himself with his philosophy.

Anne's legacy to her people is not easy to define. Most obviously, if incongruously, the homely Queen presided over a nation victorious in arms to a degree unknown since Henry V, and to be unequalled until the feats of Wellington. Anne's reign was one of almost continuous warfare: the names of Blenheim, Ramillies, Oudenarde and Malplaquet remind us that British history was being shaped on foreign battlefields. As the greatest historian of the reign, G. M. Trevelyan, has written:

> The story of the reign of Queen Anne is no parochial theme. It involves great issues, moves among brilliant societies, and reveals distant landscapes. Whoever writes of the England of that day must show Marlborough's many-coloured columns winding along the banks of Rhine, Danube and Maas; English fleets heaving on Mediterranean and Biscayan waters, or coasting the West Indian islands and the misty Newfoundland shore; Gibraltar's rock rising into azure above unwonted smoke and uproar; envoys posting over land and ocean with Godolphin's gold and Marlborough's persuasive counsel to half the Courts of Europe from Lisbon to Moscow.

At the end of it all, the Sun King had failed in his misguided attempt to subjugate Europe by force of arms: if the sixteenth century was that of Spain, and the seventeenth century that of France, the fact that in the eighteenth century there was no one Continental power bidding for supremacy was due, in no small measure, to those victories won by Marlborough for Queen Anne.

Success on the battlefield was consolidated by the triumphs of the diplomats. The treaty of Utrecht, concluded the year before Anne's death, marked for Louis the end of his grand design: and for Great Britain a signpost towards her imperial future. France was forced to concede that the Crowns of France and Spain would never be united, and to renounce her claim to the Low Countries – that vital region over which Britain had fought in the Middle Ages and was to fight again in the twentieth century. And by the acquisition of new world-wide bases – in particular of Gibraltar and Port Mahon in the Mediterranean, and Newfoundland and the Hudson Bay territories in North America – her diplomats ensured that the

In the great wars against Louis XIV, money was a vital factor for organising and equipping the armies and fleets. England's record of naval and military success during Anne's reign was made possible by important developments in her system of public finance. One of these developments was the founding of the Bank of England on 27 July 1694 for the purpose of funding the war. This late seventeenth-century engraving shows financial transactions in one of the offices of the Bank of England.

During Anne's reign, trade and commerce flourished in England, despite the long war with France. By 1713, the Dutch as well as the French were experiencing financial decline, leaving England with unrivalled opportunity for expansion. RIGHT The London Customs House, rebuilt after the Great Fire by Sir Christopher Wren, but burned down again in 1718.

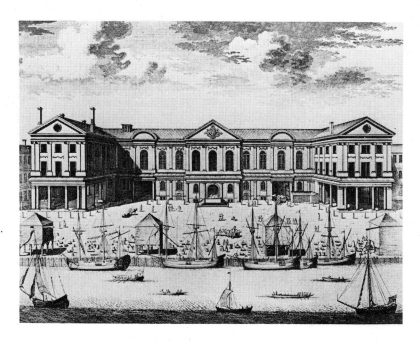

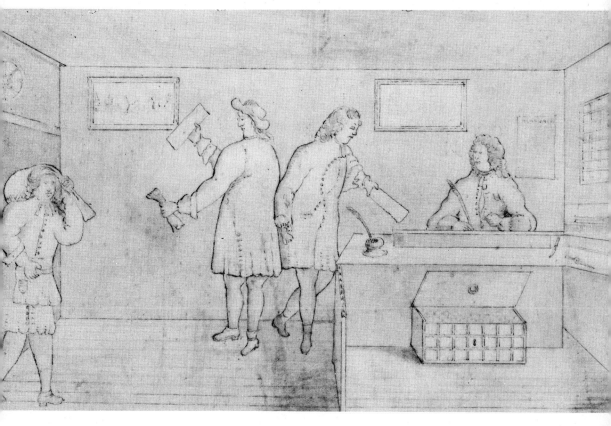

expansion begun by Raleigh in Virginia would continue on its way to create, ultimately, the largest empire the world has known, or is likely to know.

It is in some ways paradoxical that a reign dominated by war could still be characterised by economic growth. Yet the fact is that the war with France interfered little with the steadily increasing prosperity of the nation as a whole. Obviously the poor remained desperately poor, as they were to do until the twentieth century. But for the businessman and the trader, Anne's reign was one of continuous improvement and, with the decline of European rivals (the Dutch as well as the French), new opportunities. They, in turn, supplied the capital which later in the century would finance the agricultural and industrial revolutions.

It is inconceivable that all this could have happened without some degree of confidence and stability, and here Anne's personal contribution should not be underrated. A moderate woman in her tastes and ambitions, she was not one to lead any party or faction into irreconcilable conflict with its enemy. She tried to find a *via media*, in the great Elizabethan tradition, identifying wholly with no one: the party of war or of peace, Anglican or Dissenter, Whig or Tory, Harley or Bolingbroke. She did not succeed and she had her preferences, but they never destroyed the unity of the nation. Indeed, it would have been totally alien to her temperament if they had been allowed to do so. And so, as Anne struggled to dampen party strife and to lift the Crown above it, she played her part in moving English politics away from the storms and strife of the seventeenth century into the calmer waters of the eighteenth when England's prosperity and stability would become the envy of Europe.

England's wars and Anne's own unifying influence both assisted the development of a patriotism which was more than tinged by a strident chauvinism. It was one of Anne's private physicians, John Arbuthnot, who in 1712 invented the immortal character of John Bull. He was described as 'an honest, plain-dealing Fellow, choleric, Bold and of very inconstant temper,' which he said was due to the English climate, 'for his Spirits rose and fell with the Weatherglass'. John Bull's success was immediate, for he echoed the national mood, tired of looking abroad – particularly to Paris – for its public taste. Roast

The field of painting in the late seventeenth and early eighteenth centuries was dominated by foreign artists. In portraiture, the Flemish Peter Lely was succeeded by the German Godfrey Kneller, while the most fashionable exponents of decorative painting were the Italian Antonio Verrio and the Frenchman Louis Laguerre.
LEFT Self-portrait of Antonio Verrio, a Neapolitan artist who was invited to England by Charles II, and employed in the decorating of Windsor Castle. He also carried out much of the decorative painting at Hampton Court for William III and Anne, and at Burleigh House, Stamford and Chatsworth.

beef now reigned supreme: the symbol of the wholesome English and the antithesis of the over-subtle Continental. The archetypal English squire rejoiced in his beef; he also intensely disliked foreigners, as Addison tellingly satirised in an imaginary conversation:

> ... finding him such a critic upon foreigners, I asked him, if he had ever travelled; He told me, he did not know what travelling was good for, but to teach a man to ride the great horse, to jabber French, and to talk against passive obedience: to which he added, that he scarce ever knew a Traveller in his life who had not forsook his principles, and lost his hunting seat.

The Englishman's pride in his constitution, his monarchy, his food and himself was being born in an age of complacency,

RIGHT Self-portrait of
Godfrey Kneller, who was
born in Lübeck. In 1674
he came to England at the
invitation of the Duke of
Monmouth, and was
introduced to Charles II.
He became Court painter
to Charles, a post he held
right through to the reign
of George I, and the most
fashionable portrait
painter of his day.

but of confidence. It was a confidence which permeated all aspects of the nation's cultural life, and it was Anne's reign which
saw the beginnings of the Augustan age. It was not so much
in painting, where foreigners like the German Kneller, the
Swedish Dahl, the Italian Verrio and the Frenchman Laguerre
held sway, or in music where Purcell had no great successor,
and where again it was a foreigner, Handel, who was the greatest composer to live in England under Anne. But in the work of
architects and craftsmen, English genius was everywhere
visible. While Anne was building Blenheim for Marlborough
and altering Kensington for herself, her subjects, too, were
busily commissioning new houses from their architects, ranging from the palatial dwellings of the aristocracy at Chatsworth
and Castle Howard, to the less pretentious but still beautifully

Grinling Gibbons was probably of Dutch extraction, but was certainly living in England by 1666. He was recommended by John Evelyn to Charles II, who employed him to undertake the woodcarving in the new State apartments at Windsor. He went on to execute decorative woodcarving for Wren at St Paul's, and for William III at Hampton Court, and an immense amount of ornamental work at Burleigh, Chatsworth, Petworth and other great houses.
FAR LEFT Detail of some of his carving in limewood, from the Grinling Gibbons Room at Petworth.
LEFT Godfrey Kneller's portrait of Gibbons, painted in 1690.

elegant country houses of the gentry which today, with the Classical churches of Hawksmoor and Wren, provide us with the finest tangible memorial of Anne's reign. Preoccupations with symmetry and with Classical form characterised English literature as well as English architecture. Queen Anne's reign, in fact, saw the beginnings of the Augustan Age whose greatest figure – Alexander Pope – embarked on his literary career in 1709. He set himself quite deliberately to recreate the style of the ancient masterpieces, and his use of the heroic couplet brought a new dimension to English verse. But Pope, and most of the Augustans, were not mere *litterateurs*. They were deeply

Domestic Architecture in the reign of Queen Anne

While Vanbrugh and his colleagues were producing their grandiloquent Baroque mansions for the wealthiest in the land, less fashionable architects were developing a vernacular style, derived from Dutch and traditional English elements. This style, now known as 'Queen Anne' is synonymous with quiet dignity and calm symmetry, a world away from the dramatic impact of Blenheim.

LEFT The west front of Tintinhull House in Somerset, which was added to the early seventeenth-century house in 1700.
RIGHT The entrance porch to Mompesson House, in the cathedral close at Salisbury.
BELOW Westwell in Kent. This red brick house was built for John Blackmore by an unknown artisan builder between 1711 and 1717.

involved in public controversy and debate. Swift was a Tory, while Pope, Addison and Steele were Whigs, and much of the literature of the period derives from the party feud. As the world of letters moved out of the Court and into the clubs, so the great period of political satire and pamphleteering gathered momentum. Most obviously, it found expression in journalism and particularly in the Tory *Examiner* and *Post Boy*, and their Whig counterparts – the *Observateur* and the *Post Man*. Even when, in 1711, Addison and Steele founded the *Spectator* and claimed it would publish only serious essays and would maintain a high-minded neutrality between the political parties, they

The Great Fire of 1666 destroyed eighty-seven of the City churches. A committee was accordingly set up to rebuild fifty-one of these, under the supervision of Christopher Wren, who organised the design and building of the majority of the churches in the 1670s and 1680s, though many were not completed until the 1700s.

RIGHT The steeple of
St Vedast, Foster Lane, built
by Wren and Hawksmoor
between 1694–7.
ABOVE RIGHT Wren's
steeple for Christchurch,
Newgate Street.
ABOVE LEFT The London
skyline during the reign
of Queen Anne. St Paul's
dome dominates the City,
but it is complemented by
the variety of church spires
and towers.

ABOVE Richard Steele, Addison's collaborator on the *Spectator*, and an ardent Whig. Portrait by Godfrey Kneller for the Kit-Cat Club, 1711. RIGHT Alexander Pope, the brilliant young essayist who created such a storm in 1711 on the publication of his *Essay on Criticism*. At first, he was a friend of Addison, and his work was printed in the *Spectator*, but he became estranged from the Whigs over *The Rape of the Lock* and transferred his allegiance to Swift and the Tories. Portrait by C. Jervas, *c.* 1715.

were quite unable to carry this out and soon found themselves crossing swords with the Tory *Examiner*. It was, indeed, the close involvement of literary figures in public affairs that not only added venom to party battles but also launched English journalism on a distinguished course.

The age of Anne can be viewed on both the grand and the small scale. She herself was a small-minded figure, her pre-occupations often no more than trivial. The achievements of her reign were often grandiose and, indeed, heroic. Each level complemented the other and is equally characteristic. To some, Anne's memorial may be the victory at Blenheim and the great Palace to which it gave its name; to others the most enduring memory would be the busy craftsman at his elegant woodwork, or the daily round of the Queen herself, writing those bizarre letters to her dear Mrs Freeman.

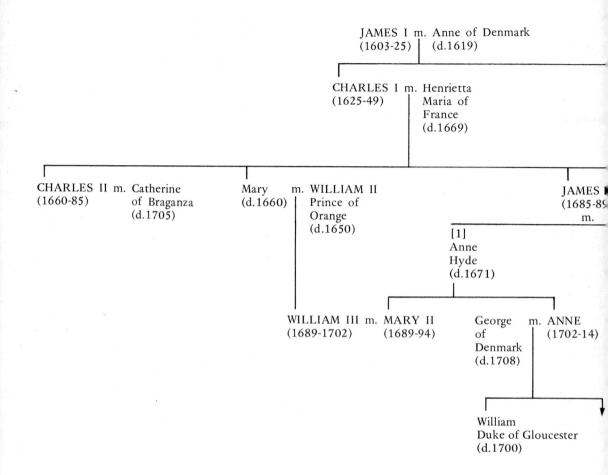

JAMES I m. Anne of Denmark
(1603-25) (d.1619)

CHARLES I m. Henrietta
(1625-49) Maria of
France
(d.1669)

CHARLES II m. Catherine
(1660-85) of Braganza
(d.1705)

Mary m. WILLIAM II
(d.1660) Prince of
Orange
(d.1650)

JAMES
(1685-89
m.

[1]
Anne
Hyde
(d.1671)

WILLIAM III m. MARY II
(1689-1702) (1689-94)

George m. ANNE
of (1702-14)
Denmark
(d.1708)

William
Duke of Gloucester
(d.1700)

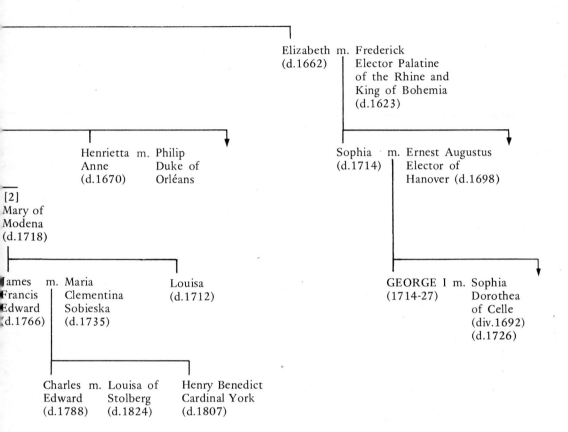

Elizabeth m. Frederick
(d.1662) | Elector Palatine
of the Rhine and
King of Bohemia
(d.1623)

Henrietta m. Philip
Anne | Duke of
(d.1670) | Orléans

Sophia m. Ernest Augustus
(d.1714) | Elector of
Hanover (d.1698)

[2]
Mary of
Modena
(d.1718)

James m. Maria
Francis | Clementina
Edward | Sobieska
(d.1766) | (d.1735)

Louisa
(d.1712)

GEORGE I m. Sophia
(1714-27) | Dorothea
of Celle
(div.1692)
(d.1726)

Charles m. Louisa of
Edward | Stolberg
(d.1788) | (d.1824)

Henry Benedict
Cardinal York
(d.1807)

Select bibliography

Ashley, Maurice, *Charles II* (1971)

Ashton, J., *Social Life in the Reign of Queen Anne* (1882)

Boyer, Abel, *History of the Reign of Queen Anne digested into Annals* (1703–13)

Brown, Beatrice Curtis, *The Letters of Queen Anne* (1935)

Chapman, Hester, *Queen Anne's Son* (1954)

Churchill, Sir Winston, *Marlborough, His Life and Times* (1947)

Clark, G. N., *The Later Stuarts* (Oxford History of England, 2nd edition 1955)

Clerke, J. S., *The Life of James II* (1816)

Connell, Neville, *Anne, the last Stuart Monarch* (1937)

Evelyn, John, *Diary* (ed. de Beer, 1955)

Feiling, Sir Keith, *History of the Tory Party* (1924)

Green, David, *Blenheim Palace* (1951)
  Gardener to Queen Anne (1956)
  Sarah, Duchess of Marlborough (1967)
  Queen Anne (1970)

Hamilton, Lady Elizabeth, *The Backstairs Dragon* (1969)

Holmes, Geoffrey, *British Politics in the Age of Anne* (1967)

Hopkinson, M. R., *Anne of England* (1934)

Lever, Sir Tresham, *Godolphin, His Life and Times* (1952)

Marlborough, Sarah, Duchess of, *An Account of the Conduct of the Dowager Duchess of Marlborough* (ed. Hooke, 1742)

Oman, Carola, *Mary of Modena* (1962)

Plumb, J. H., *The Growth of Political Stability in England* (1967)

Rowse, A. L., *The Early Churchills* (1956)

Swift, Jonathan, *Journal to Stella* (ed. Williams, 2 vols., 1948)

Trevelyan, G. M., *England under Queen Anne* (3 vols., 1930–34)

Index

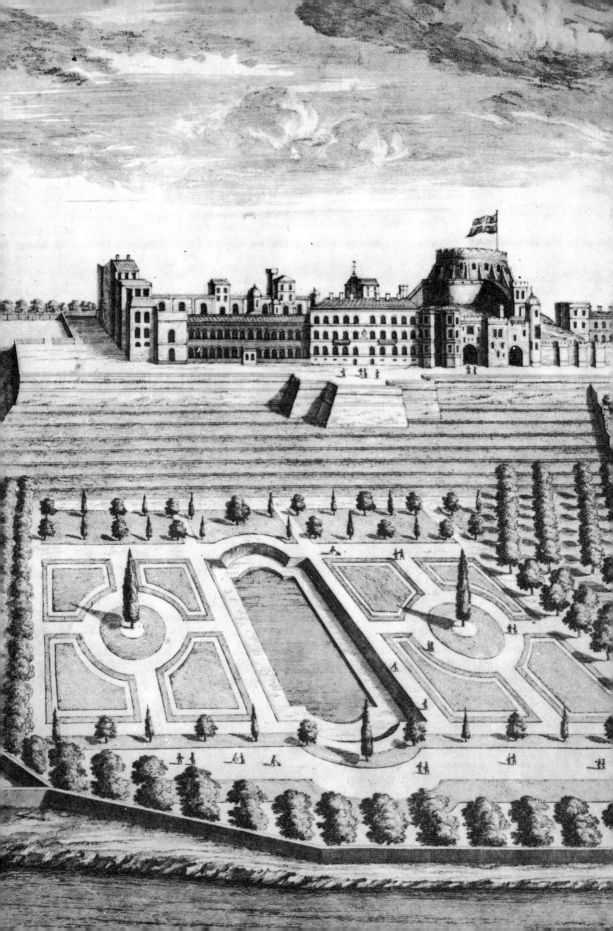